The Labour Relations Commission Seminar Series

NEW CHALLENGES TO IRISH INDUSTRIAL RELATIONS

Edited for the Labour Relations Commission by
Patrick Gunnigle and William K. Roche

Oak Tree Press

Dublin
in association with
The Labour Relations Commission

Oak Tree Press
4 Arran Quay, Dublin 7
a division of Cork Publishing Limited

© 1995 Labour Relations Commission

ISBN 1-872853-82-X (pbk.)

Printed in Ireland by Colour Books Ltd.

THE LABOUR RELATIONS COMMISSION
SEMINAR SERIES

1. "The Management of Change — Experiences, Practices, Procedures" (Cork, May 1993).

2. "World Class Manufacturing — Implications for Work Practices and Employment" (Waterford, November 1993).

3. "Competitiveness and Employment in Europe — Implications for Industrial Relations" (Galway, April 1994).

Contents

III
COMPETITIVENESS AND EMPLOYMENT IN EUROPE

Foreword

As part of the Labour Relations Commission's remit of encouraging a positive and constructive approach to industrial relations, it is centrally concerned with the development of good industrial relations. The Commission therefore in pursuance of its statutory remit of promoting an improvement in our industrial relations climate decided to organise a number of seminars throughout the country on issues of broad and continuing concern to industrial relations practitioners.

The background to the topics of the seminar series reflects the changing nature of employment and its organisation, and the opportunities, pressures and problems which emerge from such continuing changes.

Possibly the most critical contemporary development impacting on industrial relations practice is the intensification of competitive pressures on organisations. Factors such as increased international trade, competition from the emerging Asian and former communist bloc economies and developments in technology and communications are forcing organisations to adopt change initiatives at an accelerating pace. From an industrial relations perspective a key issue is the implementation of such change initiatives in a fashion which both enhances competitiveness and maintains industrial relations cohesion.

Throughout the 1980s and continuing into the 1990s changes in Irish industry and in public and commercial services mirror developments in the global marketplace. As an open and export-oriented economy, Irish industry and services have felt the full impact of these continuing and radical changes. Management and unions have had to cope with new theories of work organisation, intense competitive pressures, the locations and relocation of industries, new forms of ownership, deregulation, labour law changes, the continuing impact of production and information technology and the preservation and creation of employment.

The Labour Relations Commission Seminar Series was initiated by the Commission to provide a forum for employers, trade unions and policy makers to engage these various challenges in industrial relations. Seminars were conducted at venues in Cork, Waterford and Galway which respectively addressed the themes of (i) the management of change; (ii) world class manufacturing and its implications for work practices and employment, and (iii) competitiveness and employment in Europe. Prominent speakers from industry, trade unions, the public sector, academia, Government and the European Union were invited to present papers and debate these issues with a range of industrial relations practitioners.

This book synthesises the debate stimulated through the Seminar Series by presenting the papers delivered and placing these in the broader context of competitive pressures and their challenge to industrial relations practice. This work is very much in line with the Labour Relations Commission's policy of adopting a proactive stance on industrial relations issues and in facilitating constructive dialogue on such issues between all sides of industry. This is reflected also by the more proactive role of the Commission's conciliation service and by the development of a new and extensive advisory service.

The Labour Relations Commission is grateful to all of the speakers who addressed the individual seminars. It wishes to thank Professor Bill Roche (UCD) and Patrick Gunnigle (University of Limerick) for their professional assistance in editing this series.

The Commission also wishes to express its gratitude in particular to the European Commissioner for Social Affairs, Mr Padraig Flynn, for addressing the seminar in Galway and to the European Commission for its assistance in funding that seminar.

Finally, no seminar can be successful without a good chairperson and the Commission wishes to express its sincere appreciation to Professor Denis Lucey (University College Cork) who performed that task at all of our seminars.

Kieran Mulvey
Chief Executive

1

Competition and the New Industrial Relations Agenda

William K. Roche
Director of Research,
Graduate School of Business,
University College Dublin

Patrick Gunnigle
Department of Personnel and
Employment Relations, University of Limerick

INTRODUCTION

The contributions to this book, and to the seminar series on which the book is based, deal in different ways with challenges to traditional or established industrial relations practices in Ireland. These challenges arise from such major forces as intensified international competition, changes to the structure of product and service markets, European integration and new approaches to the management of manufacturing technologies. Their impact is evident in attempts by companies to manage change successfully and with minimum disruption; in efforts by trade unions, employer organisations and international agencies to analyse and control changes in line with their own agendas; and in workplace initiatives aimed at restructuring — sometimes profoundly — production systems and working practices.

In dealing with these major themes the book follows the seminar series in its division into three sections. Section I deals with the management of change at the level of the company and the workplace. Section II deals with the impact of development in the European Union and the wider international arena on industrial relations. Section III examines the implications for the conduct of industrial relations of new manufacturing concepts, in particular, World Class Manufacturing.

Contributions to the book fall into three broad categories. Some contributors adopt a panoramic view, seeking to sketch the nature and direction of international economic and industrial trends and to draw out their implications for the conduct of industrial relations. Others present more detailed discussions of central concerns to companies in the light of such trends, for example, how corporate strategy may be developed and implemented in a context of change, how new principles of organisational design are being adopted, and what the implications of new manufacturing concepts may be for work and employment. Finally, several contributors concentrate on the presentation of case studies of the practical impact on particular companies of new trends and management's and union responses.[*]

In this chapter we seek to provide a backdrop for the contributions to the book by examining first, the nature of the major external trends now impacting on the conduct of industrial relations in Ireland and second, the main lines of management and union response apparent at company and workplace levels.

EXTERNAL CHALLENGES TO ESTABLISHED INDUSTRIAL RELATIONS PRACTICE

In Beaumont's contribution to this book he stresses that the main forces making for change in industrial relations practice in the countries of the European Union originate *outside* the sphere of industrial relations in international commercial, political and technological trends. These trends are touched on by a number of contributors. They provide the major focus of Tony Hubert's and Commissioner Padraig Flynn's contributions and frame the contributions of John Dunne, sketching the employer's perspective on future lines of industrial relations in Europe and Peter Cassells' contribution on the trade union perspective. These contributors set their discussions of indus-

---

[*] In editing seminar contributions for publication we have tried to retain as much as possible of the original texts prepared for oral presentation. However, as prose styles geared to oral presentation do not always translate well to the inanimate medium of a book, some changes have been necessary. We have tried to restrict these to the removal of passages and graphics clearly written with a view to oral delivery, to the avoidance of repetition, and to reworking, where possible, points in the text which presenters intended to expand upon in their presentations but which without such extemporisation are obscure or incomplete.

trial relations in the context of an analysis of international competitiveness and European policies to a degree that would have been inconceivable in the past in discussions of industrial relations practice.

Never before has the analysis of industrial relations practices and policies been so closely tied to an appreciation of commercial and national and international political pressures. In the past, the worlds of industrial relations practitioners and academics alike tended to be much more introverted and preoccupied with the internal dynamics of industrial relations systems, agreements and procedures. The professional preoccupations and vocabularies of industrial relations experts tended to revolve around distinctly industrial relations themes: disputes and grievance procedures, anomalies in pay structures, productivity bargaining, inter-union bargaining groups etc. Currently, these concerns, though not altogether displaced, often take second place to such issues as company performance, the union's role in contributing to business success, mission statements and quality standards, business units, employment flexibility and so on.

It may be useful to focus here on two major external forces underpinning a number of contributions to the book: (a) the intensification of international competition, and (b) changes in governance and the regulation of the public sector.

Intensified Competition

One of the key trends in business of the past two decades has been the globalisation of competition in product, service and capital markets. This has arisen from developments in transport and communications infrastructures, but much more importantly from the liberalisation of world trade. The evolving process of European integration, culminating in the European single market, the liberal trade policy of GATT, the emergence of Japan and the Pacific Rim countries as major trading nations and, latterly, the disintegration of the former Eastern block and increasing integration of former communist-dominated nations into international trade have led to intensified international competition across a range of product and service markets. These developments have been of particular importance for Ireland, given both the "smallness" and the extreme "openness" of the Irish economy. Ireland's reliance on international trade exposes its highly significant exporting sectors to global competition, even allowing that foreign companies dominate Irish industrial exports and that the degree to which competitiveness revolves crucially around cost/price considerations, as distinct from considerations of quality or innovation, varies across product markets and over time (McAleese and Gallagher, 1994; NESC, 1993: ch. 4).

A significant theme in reviews of Irish industrial relations during the 1970s and early 1980s was the apparent willingness of foreign-owned firms to concede wage increases above levels set down in national wage agreements or higher than the norms emerging in decentralised pay rounds (Hardiman, 1988; Roche and Geary, 1994). Given the capacity of foreign-owned firms to absorb labour-cost rises, the major unions often targeted such companies in the early stages of pay rounds. The available evidence for the period since the late 1980s suggests that foreign-owned firms in general, many possibly facing much tougher international price competition, now tend to settle within prevailing wage norms (Roche and Geary, 1994). In many cases this may reflect a change in corporate strategy and organisation in parent companies which involves plants competing against each other for business and new investment. When multinational companies are configured in this way, local plants must have regard to the cost structures of their facility as compared with other plants in the company or even competing with the company. This provides a direct incentive towards cost control and can lead to tight control of the pay bill, especially in labour intensive industries. Perhaps related to this development, unions for their part have seemed less able — though in the context of the prevailing national wage programmes they may also have been less willing — to focus their bargaining efforts on major foreign-owned companies to win concessions that might set headlines for other employers.

An illustration of how even high-tech foreign companies in Ireland, not originally competing primarily on cost grounds, can face intensified price competition can be found in the severe competitive squeeze experienced by computer companies like Digital and Ahmdahl in the early 1990s. Another instructive example of price and cost becoming pivotal, with major implications for industrial relations, is provided by Syntex Ireland, which in 1993 faced possible closure following the expiry of the patent on a highly successful drug manufactured by its parent company, the Syntex Corporation. The County Clare plant found itself competing for survival with Syntex plants in other countries. The price of survival was a major overhaul in cost structures and radical changes in industrial relations practices (IRN, 1993).

A more recent example is provided by Packard Electric in Tallaght, a subsidiary of General Motors, which faced a competitive threat to its survival emanating from its cost structure relative to other Packard plants in Europe, including a plant located in Eastern Germany. At Labour Court hearings into the dispute, Packard management claimed that the Tallaght plant was 20 per cent less efficient than Packard plants in Spain, Portugal and Turkey. Again, survival turned on containing pay costs and accepting changes in working practices, geared to increasing productivity, at the Tallaght plant. While the IDA has been urged by the Government to concentrate their job creation efforts in industries not open to such a degree as engineering and electronics to price and cost competition from low-cost European economies, it is clear from the recent industrial history of foreign-owned firms in Ireland that considerations of cost can prove crucial to the survival and growth in Ireland of major companies.

For indigenous Irish companies producing for export markets cost considerations are usually of greater significance in maintaining competitiveness. This is because indigenous firms more often sell price-sensitive products. The clothing industry provides a particularly stark illustration of the impact of intensified international competition on both export and domestic markets on job security. In this sector, marginal changes in the tax regimes of competing countries, like the UK, or movements in exchange rates, may pose severe competitive pressure on exports. For indigenous exporters the structural features associated with the "smallness" of the Irish economy pose particular problems in the context of intensified competition. Relatively small-scale production units and lack of management expertise in such areas as marketing, may limit the ability of companies to respond to price competition by cutting costs; restrict their scope to diversify markets geographically, or prevent them from seeking to move to less price-sensitive market segments (McAleese and Gallagher, 1994; Kennedy et al., 1988).

Irish firms producing for the domestic market also face intensified competition in which considerations of price are frequently of major importance. It has been pointed out that frequently Irish imports are non-competitive with domestic producers (McAleese and Gallagher, 1994: 25). Nevertheless, in many product markets, particularly consumer markets such as those in food and clothing, domestic producers now face direct competition with products produced throughout the world. Indigenous suppliers of components and related products to foreign-owned companies operating in Ireland must also maintain competitiveness relative to other potential suppliers abroad. With the completion of the Single Market, the coming into force of EU measures to liberalise trade in services will also expose domestic providers of services in areas like banking and financial services to unprecedented levels of competition — adding further to the already intensified domestic competition between providers of such services resulting from the deregulation of these industries during the 1980s. The recent coming into force of EU regulations on the public procurement market also means that domestic suppliers of goods and services to organisations in the Irish public domain must now compete for business with suppliers elsewhere in the EU. The loss by a Smurfit printing subsidiary of the contract to produce directories for Telecom Éireannn at the close of 1994 sent shock waves through Irish business. The success of a foreign competitor highlighted the changed competitive conditions facing domestic producers of goods and services for what had long been a protected and stable market. It has been pointed out that the same structural features which limit the competitive performance of Irish exporters pose major competitive challenges for companies in exposed domestic markets (Kennedy et al., 1988: chs. 11-12).

Even in the case of products and markets where pressures on cost are not so intense and competitiveness revolves to a greater degree around considerations of product or service quality (or novelty/innovation), intensified international competition carries major implications for industrial relations practices.

The strategy of explicitly focusing on the quality or intrinsic features of products or services as a means of securing sustainable competitive advantage, and hence of making competitiveness less sensitive to considerations of price and cost alone, is a major international business trend of the past two decades. Competitive postures based on quality and product innovation originated in leading international companies in manufacturing industries like motor manufacturing and electronics and service industries like airline travel. Competing on the basis of quality involves the adoption by companies of exacting manufacturing standards or rigorous criteria of service quality. To realise these standards new approaches to manufacturing and service delivery are adopted, utilising techniques like quality circles, total quality management (TQM) and world-class manufacturing (WCM).

These production techniques frequently dovetail with other innovations more directly focused on cost control, for example, lean production and just-in-time production (JIT). New manufacturing concepts and techniques and new ways of producing services have now diffused well beyond the large international companies in which they were pioneered. In Ireland we find significant developments in these areas in indigenous companies, whether producing for export or domestic markets. Foreign-owned companies will frequently insist that their components and sub-assembly suppliers adopt similar standards of rigour in monitoring quality to those they themselves apply, putting pressure on small local manufacturing companies to copy the management systems and working practices of leading-edge companies. In industries like retailing, the major foreign-owned and indigenous chains now also tend to insist that suppliers of products adopt rigorous manufacturing and quality standards. The most well known example of such a strategy is that provided by Marks and Spencer.

The Industrial Policy Review Group (Culliton Committee) (1992) has enshrined in current Irish industrial policy the principle of seeking to make the development of "clusters" the cornerstone of national competitive advantage. This strategy involves giving priority to sectors and networks of companies capable of competing on the basis of indigenous skills and industrial traditions, natural advantages and other aspects of competitive advantage not easily replicable by foreign competitors. While progress towards the achievement of clusters is yet unclear, the thrust of the cluster strategy would seem to imply competing, where possible, on the basis of skills, competencies and distinctive product attributes rather than on the basis of price/cost or the manufacture of products of a generic character, which could be as easily produced in other locations. While there may be no simple correspondence between the cluster strategy and patterns of industrial relations based on high skill, strong employee commitment and flexible work practices, the viability of such a model is likely to be greater in competitive circumstances in which companies are made less vulnerable to ruthless price competition or competition based on ease of replication of product and service attributes (cf. Kochan and Dyer, 1993). If quality and distinctive product/service attributes prove easy for competitors to emulate, competition is then likely to focus on price.

In parallel to such developments in international competition and Irish industrial strategy, a number of commentators have identified a

change in the *structure* of competition in a broad range of product
and service markets. In place of competition focused on uniform
products and services there has evolved in some markets, or market segments, competition focused on the provision of customised
products or services. The *extent* of such a trend in product and
service markets remains a matter of considerable controversy in the
academic literature (see, for example, Piore and Sabel, 1984;
Streeck, 1992; Proctor et al., 1994). Commentators convinced that
this represents a major secular trend across a wide range of product
and service markets write of the emergence of "post-Fordist" markets and production systems, characterised by extensive product
differentiation, rapidly changing product lines, customisation, very
versatile production technologies, shorter production cycles, higher
levels of skill and more flexible modes of workforce deployment
and redeployment. While the extent of such a trend may be debat-
able, that major consumer product and service markets have
changed in this way cannot be doubted. Witness, for example, the
remarkable level of product diversification which has occurred in
recent years in retail banking and financial services, the diversification and short product life-cycles of cars and many consumer
durable goods and the multiplication of product varieties and product variations in retail food markets. A further example, provided
in this book by Sean Donnelly, concerns an IDA-assisted small
clothing company faced by demands for customisation and variety
from its major customer.

Changes in Governance and the Public Sector

The competitive trends identified above are now beginning to impact
in a major way on companies in the public domain. This is due
largely to the level of governance shifting in respect of economic
policy to the European Community. The effects of such a shift in the
governance of markets have been compounded by associated changes
in the posture of Irish governments towards commercial and industrial relations problems in the semi-state companies.

Traditionally the semi-state companies were strongly protected
from competition by their status as statutory monopolies. The serious
fiscal difficulties faced by Irish governments during the 1980s and
early 1990s, combined with the impact of fiscal targets set down in
the context of the Maastricht process, represented the first real pres-

sures on the cost structures of semi-state companies and their attendant managerial systems and industrial relations practices. Edward
O'Connor's contribution to this book recounts the stark situation
faced by Bord na Mona in such a climate and the way in which the
company's straitened circumstances acted as a catalyst for profound
industrial relations change.

With closer European integration and the advent of the Single
Market, these protections have been eroded, or stand to be removed
with time. Aer Lingus faced increased cost competition on hitherto
profitable routes from 1987, triggered by EU attempts to deregulate
air travel in the Community. The ESB now faces the prospect of EU-
instigated competition in the electricity market. This impending
change in the competitive circumstances faced by the Board, combined with the devastating effect of the 1991 electricians' strike, has
led to a profound change in the industrial relations ethos of the ESB
and its unions. For the first time since the Board was founded, serious
joint union-management efforts are being made to move beyond adversarial industrial relations (cf. Hastings, 1994). Telecom Éireann
still enjoys a monopoly of the domestic telephone business, but faces
stiff competition from foreign utilities providing international call
services and from domestic foreign competitors providing value-
added services other than voice telephony. In the year 2003, the company loses its derogation from European Union regulations on competition in the call services market.

The changed circumstances of Telecom Éireann have also encouraged major initiatives in industrial relations change, this time under
the broad rubric of total quality management. Like ESB, Telecom
faces the challenge of seeking to recast industrial relations practices,
while simultaneously facing job losses of considerable scale. Moreover, the company is also preparing for a strategic alliance with a
major international company in the telecommunications industry. The
change process at Telecom, like that at ESB, has led to the adoption
of non-traditional postures by the company's main union, the Communication Workers' Union. The CWU has sought to influence the
debate on Telecom's acquisition of a strategic partner. Specifically,
the union has articulated a perspective on the kind of competitive
posture best suited to respond to the changing market, while simultaneously supporting an industrial relations culture based on high skill,
progressive union-management relations and the preservation of as
many jobs as competitive conditions allow (CWU, 1984). Telecom

management have shown signs of being prepared to give the union a voice in the process of decision-making on the issue of a strategic alliance.

The shift in governance towards policies shaped at the level of the European Union has thus unleashed competitive forces in markets in which the semi-states long enjoyed a monopoly. Competition has in turn set in train a dynamic of change in industrial relations in the public domain. The main direction of change has been away from the established adversarial model towards the adoption of new concepts of partnership, consensual joint decision-making, work flexibility and product/service quality.

Changes in governance and political regulation, following on from European integration, have also impacted on the traditions of State intervention in public-sector industrial relations crises in Ireland. EU competition policy narrowed the leeway available to the Government to underwrite the survival of Irish Steel and Aer Lingus in the wake of serious commercial and industrial relations crises during 1994.

But the Government's handling of these and other disputes, in particular the dispute at TEAM Aer Lingus, also pointed towards a change in the traditional stance of ministers and politicians towards disputes in public-sector companies. European constraints aside, what emerged in the most serious public-sector disputes of 1994 was an apparent new resolve by ministers to insist that management and unions find solutions to commercial and industrial relations crises through their own efforts in direct bilateral negotiations. The long-familiar dynamic in such disputes was for both parties, but in particular the unions, to appeal to ministers, over the heads of management, to win concessions denied them by the other side. This process of "political exchange" (Ferner, 1988) had coloured the handling of major public sector disputes since the various semi-states were established.

In recent years, while the familiar postures associated with "political exchange" have not altogether disappeared, there has been a new emphasis by governments on public-sector managements and unions being responsible for the fate of their companies — even to the degree that their failure to resolve serious crises, like those at Irish Steel and Team, might lead to the closure of the companies concerned. Noting the change, Tim Hastings (1994: 42) has written of a "more hands-off approach by Government . . . in which it will leave any direct intervention until the latest possible hour". The fact that intervention at "the latest possible hour" *has* remained a feature of major semi-state disputes, such as those at Team and Irish Steel, and even of the Packard dispute in the private sector, indicates that the Government's stance remains ambiguous: more "hands off" than in the past in operational industrial relations, but "hands on" if all standard industrial relations procedures have been exhausted and major closures and serious job losses seem imminent. Thus, paradoxically while some commentators can point to the emergence of a more arms-length and harder commercial stance by governments on industrial relations in the semi-states, other commentators can point in recent years to the "politicisation" of major disputes in the public and even private sector (cf. Sheehan, 1995).

If crisis political intervention becomes a standard feature of major disputes in the public sector, it inevitably threatens to dilute the direct impact of competitive forces on industrial relations restructuring at company and workplace levels. Unions, in particular, will adjust their negotiating stances in anticipation of government intervention to stave off serious job losses and their inevitable political fall-out. The logic of the policy of encouraging management and unions to share ultimate responsibility for the commercial viability of their companies points to a very residual role for governments where serious crises are precipitated. When governments do intervene, they must act to underscore rather than dilute competitive priorities — albeit not necessarily taking sides between the specific proposals of the parties in dispute. In the event, this is essentially what occurred in the 1994 Irish Steel and TEAM Aer Lingus disputes in the public sector and the 1994-95 Packard dispute in the private sector. If such a policy gains ground and becomes standard, it will add additional impetus to the impact of competitive pressures on established industrial relations practice in the public (and the private) domain.

New trends in governance are also beginning to put pressure on established industrial relations practice in the public services. While public services, by definition, are insulated most from direct competitive pressures, they are far from being inert to the trends we have been discussing. The fiscal crisis of the Irish state during the 1980s and, latterly, the Maastricht-process guidelines on the control of public debt, have led to a greater degree of control over public spending. Given that the public-service pay bill accounts for about 40 per cent of current government spending, pay determination, work practices and industrial relations generally, inevitably come under the spotlight in a tighter fiscal regime. Thus, for virtually the first time since their inception, the various conciliation and arbitration systems are being reformed, albeit modestly so far. More major changes are under negotiation in public service grading structures and related grades in the health services and local government. While the pace of industrial relations change in these areas is currently far from dramatic, it may be further accelerated by other trends in the public service, such as the implementation of the "strategic management initiative" and wider civil service reform.

Up to now, we have emphasised the challenges to established Irish industrial relations practice posed by international competitive pressures and fiscal pressures associated with the process of European integration. What also bears emphasis, however, is the manner in which European social policy will set the parameters within which managements and unions must respond to these challenges. Possibly the most tangible manifestation of the impact of the EU on Irish industrial relations has been the considerable increase in employment legislation since the 1970s (Fitzgerald, 1995). Key aspects of current Irish employment legislation, such as that on sexual equality, have their origins in European Union directives and action plans. More recent EU developments in social policy are also likely to impact considerably on the framework of Irish labour law and industrial relations practice. The 1987 Single European Act, aimed at strengthening economic cohesion by removing barriers to competition between member states, attempts to establish a common social policy framework throughout the EU. In 1989, a Charter of Fundamental Social Rights of Workers, the Social Charter, was signed by all member states, except the United Kingdom. The Social Charter (subsequently named the "Social Chapter") was drafted as a response to the objectives set out by the Single European Act of harmonising working conditions in the EU. The attendant Social Action Programme, agreed in 1990, comprises some 49 legally binding directives and recommendations. The Social Chapter and Action Programme have been supported, with varying degrees of enthusiasm, by the Irish Government, trade unions and employers (Hourihan, 1994).

While aspects of the Social Chapter are already embedded in the Irish legislative framework, the development of EU social policy and its role in regulating labour markets are clearly issues of critical concern for policy makers and industrial relations practitioners. An issue of particular importance for industrial relations is the impact of the

Social Chapter on competitiveness (Fitzgerald, 1995). This was a central reason for the United Kingdom seeking to opt out of the Social Chapter prior to the ratification of the Maastricht Treaty. To date, some progress has been made on many of the points contained in the Social Action Programme, with the most important developments occurring with the adoption of directives covering working time, the protection of pregnant workers, the protection of young workers, health and safety, employment contracts and, most recently, on information and consultation. Reviewing the impact of the European Union on Irish industrial relations Hourihan (1994) argues that EU membership has significantly impacted on the nature of national-level collective bargaining in recent years. He suggests we may be witnessing the development of a new facet of the decision-making process affecting industrial relations, with the European Commission being afforded a role as "validator" of issues covered in national agreements. Access to EU funding is now being firmly tied to the acceptance or validation by the European Commission of policy decisions achieved at national level bargaining. Increasingly, the use of EU funds may be linked to the adoption of labour market reforms put forward by Brussels. Hourihan (1994) suggests that such developments afford the European Commission an unheralded place in the formation of labour market policies in Ireland and other member states. The degree to which EU-instigated labour market and social policies are likely to impact on national systems of industrial relations is a theme considered in Beaumont's contribution to the book.

THE RESPONSE TO INTENSIFIED COMPETITION: THE NEW INDUSTRIAL RELATIONS AGENDA AT COMPANY AND WORKPLACE LEVELS

Responding to competitive pressure — by emphasising price, quality or distinctive workforce competencies — poses major challenges to established industrial relations practice. In particular, the adoption of new production concepts and techniques, geared to competing on the basis of quality or product diversification — the development path for Ireland set out in current industrial policy — would seem to require a sea-change in traditional postures and practices by each of the social partners. Flexibility becomes of cardinal importance, particularly in the organisation and performance of work; companies must seek employee and union commitment to quality as a primary concern; existing demarcations between crafts and occupations may have to give way to multi-skilled and inter-disciplinary work teams, and employees must be encouraged to participate actively in problem solving at various levels of decision-making. The practical issues that arise in seeking to implement these principles are considered in this section and examined in different ways by a number of contributors to the book. It bears emphasis that these priorities together constitute effectively a new understanding of "good industrial relations". Traditional industrial relations practice, as emphasised in particular by Alfred Pankert's contribution to this book, revolved primarily around management and unions jointly regulating working conditions through adversarial collective bargaining. In this understanding of good industrial relations, exemplary practice resided in such things as clear and detailed agreements at company or workplace level covering pay, working conditions, staffing levels, shift arrangements and the many other exigencies of employment. Stable relations between bargaining partners on the union and management sides, which allowed ongoing compromise to ensue, were also integral to this understanding of good industrial relations; collective bargaining was its pivotal practice. The transformation of the established pattern of industrial relations in Ireland, to bring it into line with the more inclusive and demanding understanding of good industrial relations entailed by new market and production trends, will necessitate a high degree of practical consensus regarding change on the part of the social partners — and very considerable skill and resourcefulness in the management of change.

The competitive pressures to which we have alluded have resulted in recent years in a deep and pervasive management-led agenda for industrial relations change. Probably at no point since the Irish industrial relations system was established as a pillar of the economic and political framework of the State have managements felt compelled to seek such a degree of change in the conduct of industrial relations across a wide range of industries. The long familiar managerial posture of reacting to union claims and absorbing union pressure has been replaced in many sectors by a new emphasis on industrial relations restructuring. Nor have unions adopted a merely reactive posture in the face of the new managerial agenda. At central level, the ICTU, SIPTU, AEEU, CWU and other unions have engaged in a process of reappraising traditional ways of representing their members' interests. Indeed some unions, in particular the AEEU in manufacturing, claim to be taking the lead in pressing management to adopt new production concepts and associated new industrial relations practices.

The various strands of the new industrial relations agenda at company and workplace levels are covered by many contributions to the book. The contributions by Moore, Morley and Geary, which deal respectively with models of change management, new approaches to organisational and job design and new manufacturing concepts, focus on key aspects of the new industrial relations agenda. The wider, and in many respects different, understanding of good industrial relations developed in response to external pressures, also emerges clearly from the case studies of Pfizer, presented by Joe Cogan, of Bord na Mona, presented by its chief executive, Edward O'Connor, and of a number of IDA-assisted companies, presented by Sean Donnelly.

Here we present a short examination of some manifestations of change in key aspects of industrial relations postures and practices at the level of organisations. The major issues briefly considered and more extensively explored in subsequent chapters are (a) flexibility, (b) quality management initiatives, (c) employee involvement and participation and (d) the role of trade unions. Our concern in discussing these issues is to identify from the wider literature the major concerns that arise in proceeding with innovations in each area and to draw attention to any relevant existing Irish evidence on the extent and impact of the new initiatives.

Flexibility

A pervasive issue underpinning many contemporary analyses in industrial relations practice is the issue of flexibility. The essential argument is that increased competitive pressures in product markets and changes in consumer behaviour, as discussed above, are forcing organisations to become increasingly flexible in almost all aspects of their operations. Academic research and debate in this area is frequently focused around three distinct types of flexibility (Atkinson, 1984):

1. *Numerical flexibility*: incorporating extensive use of atypical employment forms which allow the organisation to take on and shed labour flexibly in line with business need;

2. *Functional Flexibility*: incorporating the ability to deploy workers across a range of jobs and tasks; and

3. *Financial Flexibility*: incorporating the ability of organisations to link decisions on basic pay levels to labour market conditions and to relate decisions on pay increases to employee or company performance.

From an industrial relations perspective the emergence of the "flexible firm" scenario is most commonly associated with the adoption of a so-called "core-periphery employment model" (Atkinson, 1984; Flood, 1990). Within this scenario the "core" is composed of full-time staff who putatively enjoy relatively secure challenging jobs with good pay and employment conditions. In the case of such staff, premium is placed on the achievement of functional flexibility. In contrast the "periphery" is seen to comprise diverse groupings of temporary, part-time and contract workers who have considerably less favourable pay and employment conditions and less job security or training and promotion opportunities. This is seen to reflect an emphasis on numerical and financial flexibility in the management of these categories of staff.

It is now generally accepted that coherent, proactive core-periphery models of industrial relations restructuring are unusual and untypical of general trends. At the same time, the evidence available for Ireland indicates a definite trend towards greater flexibility in a variety of forms (Suttle, 1988; Flood, 1990; Wickham, 1993). However, this development seems to be particularly focused on numerical flexibility.

The growing use of forms of numerical flexibility by employers can probably be explained by the combination of competitive or cost pressures and high unemployment. Chronic high unemployment means that there will be a ready availability of people willing to work in temporary, contract or part-time jobs. A 1990 survey of 200 Irish private sector and commercial semi-state companies, conducted for the European Foundation for the Improvement of Living and Working Conditions, provides the best data available on aspects of the industrial relations of numerical flexibility (Wickham, 1993). The survey found that Ireland had a relatively low incidence of part-time work, fixed-term contract work, Saturday work and evening work, compared with the major European Union countries. However, in companies where such flexible forms of working were used, they generally applied to comparable, or in the specific instance of Saturday working, relatively high, proportions of staff (Wickham, 1993: ch. 3). The survey confirmed that there had been a recent rise in the importance of non-standard employment. However, the responses of managers interviewed suggested that future growth in non-standard employment would be focused around Saturday work and evening work and confined mainly to companies in which non-standard work was already well established (Wickham, 1993: 35-7). The study indicated that companies looked to non-standard employment primarily for the direct cost advantages it was seen to bring and placed relatively little emphasis on any advantages it might hold for employees. Evidence of workforce segmentation also emerged from the study; part-time workers and workers on fixed-term contracts occupied a distinct employment track, with little prospect of movement to full-time or non-contract work (Wickham, 1993: chs. 4-6).

Data released by IDA Ireland and Forfás point to a sharp rise since the late 1980s in the growth of "atypical" employment in companies supported by both agencies (or until 1994 by the IDA). Between 1987 and 1994 part-time, temporary and sub-contract employment rose by 121 per cent in companies assisted by these agencies. Over the same period permanent employment rose by 10.5 per cent (*IRN Report*, 1994, 48; 1995, 4). Of the total of 20,700 "atypical jobs" at the end of 1994, 60 per cent were in indigenous firms assisted by Forbairt and 40 per cent in overseas firms assisted by IDA Ireland. The rate of growth in atypical employment since 1992 in IDA-assisted firms, however, was in the region of 100 per cent, while that in Forbairt-assisted firms was 38 per cent. For 1994 almost 60 per cent of all employment created in IDA-assisted foreign companies was due to new contract and temporary jobs; by the end of 1994 these jobs accounted for some 10 per cent of all employment in overseas companies and 9 per cent of total employment in foreign and domestic companies assisted by the agencies. The IDA's prognosis was for a continuing increase in the employment share of atypical jobs on the grounds that companies needed "ever greater levels of flexibility in the marketplace" (*IRN Report*, 1994, 48: 11).

Trends in non-standard employment in the public service remain to be determined in detail. However, it seems clear that in response to fiscal pressure and high unemployment there has been a significant rise in the levels of part-time, temporary and contract work. The spread of non-standard employment, including increased resort to sub-contracting, has figured prominently in industrial relations in local authorities, health and education. The issue of greater managerial flexibility in making use of non-standard contracts is also on the agenda for negotiations concerning the reform of public service grades and employment practices.

Functional flexibility is defined as the expansion of skills within a workforce, or the ability of firms to reorganise the competencies associated with jobs so that job holders are able and willing to deploy such competencies across a broad range of tasks (Gunnigle et al, 1995). This process can mean employees moving into either higher or lower skill areas or a combination of both. It is sometimes referred to as multi-skilling. The evidence on functional flexibility suggests that this form of flexibility is considerably less common than other forms of flexibility and, thus far, largely confined to tentative initiatives in the manufacturing sector (Suttle, 1988; Gunnigle and Daly, 1992). Some larger organisations have taken a number of initiatives in the area of "multi-skilling", for example, the Electricity Supply Board in the semi-state sector and Krups Engineering and Auginish Alumina in the private sector.

Early case evidence suggests that "add-skilling" or "extra-skilling" are more accurate descriptions of these developments than multi-skilling. This conclusion is based on the evidence that functional flexibility among skilled workers largely involves those categories receiving training in, or agreeing to undertake, a limited range of extra tasks in addition to their traditional trade, for example fitters undertaking some electrical/instrumentation work. There is, of course, evidence of organisations claiming to have total functional flexibility in their operations. However, such flexibility would appear to pertain largely to unskilled assembly type work where there is a minimal training requirement and it is thus relatively easy to deploy workers across a large range of (simple) tasks as required (Gunnigle and Morley, 1992). A major headline initiative in the area of "complete flexibility" emerged in 1994 out of negotiations between Analog Devices and SIPTU. The "flexibility agreement" concluded at the electronics company was critical in assuring parent-company investment in a new Limerick plant in the face of competition from other Analog plants in the Far East (*IRN Report*, 1995, 2). The agreement provides, *inter alia*, for total flexibility, involving no demarcations between jobs and recognises that all jobs can expand through training and the acquisition of skills. Flexibility is also seen to entail employee involvement in both the direct work process and in preventative maintenance and the handling of breakdowns. The union is also given a voice in the company's business plan.

Financial flexibility incorporates the ability of organisations to adjust pay rates to reflect labour market conditions and to make pay increases contingent on employee performance. Financial flexibility may be used to encourage functional flexibility (Atkinson, 1984; Keenan and Thom, 1988). It is difficult to identify a clear picture for Ireland in the area of financial flexibility. Findings from the Price Waterhouse Cranfield Project suggest a trend towards the increased incidence of financial flexibility through a growth in the use of variable pay systems (Gunnigle et al, 1994; Brewster et al, 1994). However, when the incidence of performance-related pay systems across different employee categories is examined, the picture that emerges is much more traditional: the evidence suggesting that performance-related pay systems remain largely confined to managerial and professional categories of employees.

With regard to the second aspect of financial flexibility, namely adjusting base pay levels to product and labour market conditions, a number of developments are notable. First, "two-tier" pay systems have been developed in some major industries. The most prominent examples are found in banking and Aer Lingus (Flood, 1989). These initiatives involved the introduction of a new entry grade at pay levels considerably below levels pertaining to employees who traditionally carried out entry-grade work. Again, the twin pressures of more intense competition and high unemployment explain the origin of two-tier pay systems in these industries. There is little empirical evidence of a widespread incidence of this form of flexibility, although it is apparent that the current state of the Irish labour market facilitates the adoption of such initiatives.

A trend towards greater flexibility in pay was also evident during the period from the early 1980s to 1987, when pay rises negotiated in decentralised pay rounds varied significantly from company to company and sector to sector in response to competitive pressures. In previous periods of free-for-all pay bargaining, "comparability" had come to play an increasingly dominant role in the dynamics of pay determination, with the result that pay rises across a wide industrial front were contained within a narrow range. In the early to mid-1980s, the force of "fair comparisons" declined in favour of ability to pay and profitability, resulting in growing wage dispersion (see Roche, 1994a). Since the advent of the national programmes in 1987, greater uniformity has been imposed on basic pay round increases. As such, the scope for practising financial flexibility, by basing annual or periodic pay rises on considerations of company performance, has been curtailed. Under the Programme for Economic and Social Progress (1991-93), a local bargaining clause permitted negotiations at company level for a 3 per cent pay rise. It appears that the round of local negotiations frequently resulted in pay rises — sometimes well in excess of 3 per cent — linked either to blanket union commitments to "accept or co-operate with flexibility", or to specific flexibility initiatives like multi-skilling and team-working. A SIPTU survey of the union's bargaining units found that 164 companies out of 311 won concessions on flexibility as a *quid pro quo* for conceding pay rises under PESP local bargaining (SIPTU, 1993).

Under the current Programme for Competitiveness and Work less explicit scope is permitted for local bargaining. In consequence, the willingness of companies to utilise performance-related pay and other "contingent compensation systems", like skill-based pay and profit sharing, has a major bearing on the practice of financial flexibility. Initiatives in grade and category restructuring can also be used — at least on a once-off basis — as a way of adjusting pay structures to perceived market imperatives.

Much industrial relations activity and many of the most serious industrial disputes of the late 1980s and early 1990s have involved managements insisting on the revision of existing agreements and working practices. Indeed, in no other area has the management-led agenda of change been so apparent than in concession bargaining of this type which involves revisions to working conditions without compensation.

While unions across a broad industrial front have been forced to yield significant concessions with respect to working practices and conditions, concession bargaining, involving negotiated pay cuts, or downward pay flexibility, remains unusual in Irish industrial relations. This type of concession bargaining is not, however, unknown. In recent years a number of major companies have concluded agreements with unions incorporating pay cuts and pay freezes in circumstances of serious competitive difficulty. In Waterford Crystal, for example, a pay cut and long-term pay freeze were agreed as part of the company's plan for survival and recovery. Pay cuts have also been agreed in De Beers and Krups Engineering (craft workers). Cuts were mooted in other major disputes related to restructuring, for example,

TEAM and Packard, but disappeared from the negotiating agenda to be replaced by other concessions.

Given the limited incidence, thus far, of concession bargaining focused on downward pay flexibility, it would be invalid to speak of a trend in this type of financial flexibility. However, even the incidences recorded are significant in an industrial relations context long characterised by "real wage resistance", involving staunch union defence of real pay levels. Concession bargaining has become an employer option in circumstances of serious competitive difficulty and unions have been forced to accept wage cuts or freezes long viewed as unattainable in Irish industrial relations. Nor have unions in Ireland usually managed to achieve significant lasting concessions in managerial approaches or policies in return for agreeing wage cuts, or freezes or changes in working practices. Exceptions are Aer Lingus, where employee shareholding was conceded, and Waterford Crystal, where the company committed itself to a "job replacement initiative" based on developing a new packaging project and unions were given a voice in a joint task force established to review margins on products that might be subject to outsourcing.

Overall the research evidence suggests that while all forms of flexibility outlined above are on the increase, this is occurring in a somewhat piecemeal form, in reaction to depressed labour and product market conditions, rather than as part of the planned emergence of the "totally flexible firm". Such apparently expedient responses to environmental conditions may well be sustained when the environment changes and organisations seek to retain the advantages of flexibility in its various forms.

Enhanced Quality Initiatives

Over the last decade one of the most significant issues for many organisations has been a concern to achieve improvements in product quality and service. This focus is largely related to managerial desires to improve the competitive position of their organisations in the face of increased international competition. Some commentators have characterised such developments as a "Japanisation" of work practices, since it appears that the Japanese companies have often been the catalyst for the adoption of many so-called "total quality management" (TQM) or "world-class manufacturing" (WCM) techniques (Blyton and Turnbull, 1992).

In spite of their widespread currency, concepts such as TQM and WCM remain somewhat amorphous and appear to have differing meanings in different organisational contexts. For example, in some organisations TQM simply encompasses the adoption of selected techniques such as Statistical Process Control (SPC) or just-in-time (JIT) production methods. In others, TQM is a much broader concept, encompassing a total re-orientation of managerial strategy, organisational structure and job design, incorporating, for example, increased employee involvement and autonomy.

In its broadest sense, TQM involves such practices as "lean production", "cellular manufacturing", teamwork, autonomous work groups, self-inspection, total preventative maintenance, statistical process control and just-in-time systems of production and service provision (McMahon, 1995). Such systems are generally associated with functional and numerical flexibility, as discussed above. Under a TQM system, greater responsibility for quality is assigned to individual employees. TQM generally encompasses a strong emphasis on achieving continuous improvements in performance (Wilkinson, 1992). Early research evidence suggests that organisations successfully introducing TQM have found that the costs incurred during implementation are outweighed by the eventual cost savings (Hogg, 1990). Particular areas of cost savings include reduced physical costs in terms of lower inventory, reduced recalls and fewer corrections/replacements. It might also be expected that lower labour costs should materialise where organisations are discovering ways of increasing production, or improving service. It has been suggested that TQM approaches may be associated with more intense work systems and even higher levels of monitoring of employee performance (Blyton and Turnbull, 1992; Geary, 1994; Gunnigle, 1994). Thus, quality enhancement approaches often incorporate a "more with less" focus, whereby organisations seek concurrently to achieve increased productivity and lower employment levels. This has obvious implications for industrial relations. For example, it could mean that employment conditions may deteriorate, while the standards and performance expected from workers increases.

It is suggested that the main distinguishing feature of the "TQM organisation" is that quality is seen as a strategic issue rather than an operational one (McMahon, 1995). Interest in "quality" as a company orientation in Ireland is reflected by the fact that by the end of 1993, over 1,000 companies had been registered to the ISO 9000 standard (an international quality benchmark) by the National Standards Authority of Ireland (EOLAS, 1993).The growing interest of companies in quality may reflect national survey findings which claim that "people regard quality as the most important feature when buying a product" (IQA, 1994). Separate survey findings across a sample of Irish service companies reveal that "quality significantly overshadowed price in competitive pressures" — 86 per cent affirming the primacy of quality versus 14 per cent affirming the primacy of price (IQA, 1994).

Despite many of the espoused advantages of TQM and related approaches, it appears from the international literature that many organisations which have experimented in this sphere have not been particularly successful. One possible reason is that the majority of organisations which have pursued TQM initiatives have done so on a selective basis by essentially "cherry picking" particular techniques, such as SPC, and have found that the overall impact on performance of single techniques has been quite limited (McMahon, 1995). Research evidence in Britain suggests that there are extremely few organisations which adopt a "total" approach to quality management (Wilkinson, 1992; Brewster, 1992). Furthermore, only 8 per cent of British managers surveyed in a 1993 study rated their quality initiatives as totally successful (Wilkinson et al., 1993). Indeed the majority claimed only a moderate degree of success or were neutral about such practices. It is suggested that the main reasons for this are to be found in the challenge posed by TQM to existing corporate cultures. According to Wilkinson (1992), this is reflected in a preoccupation with: (a) an overly short-term focus; (b) a suggestion that requisite changes in organisational structure are difficult to implement in practice; (c) a lack of management support, particularly in relation to the devolution of autonomy to employees and (d) a lack of employee support, reflecting low levels of trust between management and employees or trade unions.

Consequently, it is hardly surprising that instances of failed initiatives with "quality" and "new forms of work organisation" have been identified in Ireland in circumstances where "relationships were characterised by low trust and a traditional adversarial approach" (ICTU, 1993). Indeed, given the "strikingly low levels of trust" which characterise worker perceptions of management in many Irish organisations (Whelan, 1982), the successful introduction of TQM approaches poses a considerable challenge to management. From an

industrial relations perspective, it is apparent that the pressures created by JIT and TQM towards lower staffing levels and more intensive work systems demand an active and co-operative workforce. For
example, given the absence of buffer stocks in the JIT environment,
and the focus on continuous improvement under a TQM regime,
there is an acute management dependence on labour co-operation.
Dependence on labour co-operation is lower when stock levels protect management from short-term production disruptions, or when the
same product (or service) can be produced (or supplied) in the same
way for years on end, without any real fear of losing market share to
higher quality or more effective competitors (Turnbull, 1988; Wilkinson and Oliver, 1990).

There is also considerable debate on the extent to which TQM
initiatives impact on employee involvement and autonomy. Some
commentators argue that TQM facilitates significantly increased levels of employee involvement through "worker empowerment" and
"mutual dependency". However, others argue that these approaches
are largely cosmetic and that key decisions are in practice determined
by management decree (see, for example, Klein, 1989; Sewell and
Wilkinson, 1992).

It appears that initial trade union opposition or scepticism towards
TQM and related developments has been replaced by a tacit acceptance of their inevitability. It now seems that trade unions internationally and in Ireland are attempting actively to engage these developments through addressing many traditional trade union concerns
about increasing industrial democracy and improving the quality of
work life. The Irish Congress of Trade Unions' 1993 policy document, *New Forms of Work Organisation*, identified a series of possible trade union responses to quality initiatives and related developments, ranging from outright opposition, through scepticism and
pragmatism, to shaping the agenda by entering "partnership" with
companies, while safeguarding trade union concerns (ICTU, 1993).
The ICTU document concluded that the most effective trade union
response was to adopt a "flexible and supportive approach", attempting to optimise the outcome for both workers and their employing
organisations. The ICTU strategy further argues for moving, wher-
ever possible, from an adversarial approach, focusing on pay and
conditions, to a "new role" as business partner. Such a shift of emphasis clearly requires, and is seen to require, a different trade union
orientation. ICTU policy on the union response to quality and related

initiatives has been informed by unions' company-level experience of these employer initiatives in practice (ICTU, 1993: ch. 5). While such things as the Q-Mark and ISO standards appear to have diffused widely across Irish industry and services, there is little evidence that the new managerial concern with quality has resulted in any radical restructuring of work and industrial relations practices based on a shared concept of "partnership". Cases like Aer Rianta, where quality initiatives did impact on traditional practices, and Analog Devices, where quality and flexibility are associated with non-traditional forms of industrial relations, remain headlines because they are still so untypical of standard practice.

Employee Involvement and Participation

The above discussion of TQM and developments in work organisation noted that many of these initiatives incorporate a focus on increased employee involvement and participation. Employee involvement and participation range from policies designed to give employees, either individually or in groups, more direct control over the performance of their jobs, to mechanisms designed to increase employee or union input into managerial decision making (Gunnigle et al., 1995).

The prescriptive industrial relations and human resource management literature suggested that all parties involved in employee relations can benefit from increased employee participation (Beer et al., 1984). For example, it is suggested that employers need a flexible and committed workforce willing to respond to change and perform at high levels of productivity with minimum levels of supervision and that this can best be achieved through employee involvement/ participation initiatives. From an employee perspective it is suggested that the achievement of an input into decisions which affect their working lives, allowing employees greater control and discretion in their jobs, is a widely desired employee goal, (Hackman and Oldham, 1980). Even at the macro level, it has been asserted that the State, the community and macro-economic performance may benefit from positive workplace relations based on trust, open communications, and employee involvement (Beer et al, 1984; Kochan and Osterman, 1994).

However, the achievement of real and effective participation within organisations remains problematic (Marchington and Parker, 1990; Salaman, 1992; Marchington, 1994). Employers, for example, argue that business confidence and managerial control of decision-making must be maintained to encourage investment and expansion. At the same time they are wont to suggest that barriers to worker involvement must be removed and employees given a worthwhile say in decision-making. This perspective is commonly used to encourage employee involvement in shop floor issues, while legitimising the retention of management prerogative in higher level business decision-making (Gunnigle and Morley, 1992).

Job or work participation encompasses various initiatives to design jobs and work systems which allow for greater individual employee involvement in decisions affecting their jobs and immediate work environment. This appears to be a most practical type of employee participation, but it can be difficult to effect successfully (Marchington, 1994). Increased employee participation in job or work-related decision-making requires effective, two-way communications between management and employees, based on mutual trust. Such initiatives are likely to succeed only where workers feel they have a valuable input to make and where that input is recognised and valued by the organisation's management. It also demands a more flexible and open approach to the management process, with less emphasis on direction and supervision and more on co-ordination and communication. This form of employee participation also involves an element of role reversal with superiors listening to employee comments, discussing these with top management and consulting employees on decisions. Approaches to employee involvement at this level may take a variety of forms such as job enlargement, autonomous work groups, quality circles, suggestion schemes, consultative meetings and "management by objectives".

Employee Participation in the wider process of company decision-making may range from the relatively superficial level of management informing employees of decisions which affect them, to consultation with employees, or their trade union representatives, on major issues of company performance, like product development, work process changes and business plans. Consultation of this kind can be given effect through project teams, consultative committees, works councils and board-level representation. Employee involvement and participation are also conventionally understood to refer to profit sharing and employee equity participation, which we have discussed above under the heading of flexibility.

While instances of all such approaches to employee involvement and participation are to be found in Irish industrial relations, progress in these areas remains piecemeal and the pace of change again appears to be slow. Employee involvement in job and work performance is commonly utilised as part of — as yet confined — initiatives to refashion work practices and industrial relations processes under the broad rubric of TQM or WCM. A study of employee involvement in the introduction of new information technology in 38 Irish establishments, conducted in the late 1980s, established that little involvement other than the basic provision of information or consultation occurred in the planning or implementation phases. Nor did there appear to be any strong desire on the part of managers or employee representatives for more developed types of involvement based on joint decision- making or negotiation (Wallace, 1990). A recent study of the attitudes of the social partners to direct employee involvement in Europe canvassed the opinions of the social partners at central level and in the banking and manufacturing sectors in Ireland (Regalia, 1994). The study seems to point to a positive overall appreciation of "direct participation" at the level of the ICTU, but scepticism as to whether "direct participation" may always be necessary on competitive grounds; concern that direct participation might be used to bypass or weaken collective bargaining; and an awareness that direct participation faces structural and inertial constraints rooted in Irish industrial relations practice and management and employee attitudes. Similar themes recur in interviews conducted in the banking and manufacturing sectors (in manufacturing, however, only one interview was conducted with the AEEU in one US multinational). Differences in union postures also emerge. Employers at central and sectoral levels seem to view the extension of direct participation in a more unequivocally positive light; express a conviction that associated changes in work organisation are essential for competitiveness; and while underlining the barriers to direct participation, appear committed to supporting its wider introduction (Regalia, 1994).

Instances of greater or lesser degrees of actual or attempted direct union involvement in broader business decision-making can be found, for example, in ESB, Telecom Éireann, Waterford Crystal, TEAM and Analog Devices. But these remain brave experiments in a realm dominated by adversarial collective bargaining and a managerial posture which seeks to marginalise unions from major decisions on company business strategy. Frequently, unions themselves remain satisfied with their marginal status, still viewing their role exclusively in terms of challenging management decisions after they have been made.

The scope for union involvement in business planning may vary as between foreign multinationals, Irish-owned multinationals and indigenous companies. The competitive focus and ultimate fate of multinational branch plants located in Ireland is likely to be determined at corporate level where Irish unions can have little influence. Unions can still become involved in operational business planning and strategy at branch-plant level, however, as is clear from the new agreement at Analog. The degree of union leverage over Irish-owned multinationals may be somewhat greater to the degree that their Irish-based plants enjoy a more pivotal position in company strategy. Thus unions in Waterford Crystal have assumed a role in reviewing products outsourced by the company from European manufacturers to determine if their production at Waterford is consistent with similar or higher profit margins. The influence over business plans of unions in foreign or Irish-owned multinationals could be affected by European Union proposals on the establishment of works councils or other similar mechanisms for informing and consulting employees. It is proposed that companies operating in the EU with at least 1,000 employees in all and — in the current draft — at least 150 employees in each of two member states be required to establish a European works council or some other procedure to provide employees with information and a voice in business decision-making. Though assessments of the likely impact of such measures on union influence vary, it has been estimated that about 120 firms in Ireland will fall within the scope of the proposed new arrangements. (see Hourihan, 1994).

In the case of indigenous companies, particularly those in the public sector, the scope for direct union involvement in business decision-making would appear to be greatest. These companies, whether producing mainly for export or domestic markets, ultimately depend for competitive success on the performance of their Irish plants. Their business strategy will be focused more directly, if not exclusively, on Irish facilities and they may have a high level of dependence on union co-operation with business plans and their industrial relations underpinnings. In the public sector, union involvement in core business decisions can be viewed as consistent with the tradition of adopting best industrial relations practice in publicly-owned companies. Unions, for their part, are not encumbered by the problem of seeking cross-national inter-union co-operation, particularly as unions in different countries are likely to have conflicting interests in company decisions on location and new investment and closures.

A range of public policy documents have discussed the potential benefits of worker participation as far back as the early 1980s and interest in the issue rose again in 1985 when an Advisory Committee on Worker Participation was established (see Department of Labour, 1980; 1986). In the absence of consensus between the social partners on ways of realising worker participation, however, little progress was likely from the government. Unions and management each es- pouse support for employee involvement and participation initiatives, but with very different slants. Irish employers staunchly resist intro- ducing legislation to support such changes, while unions favour legis- lation, particularly in the area of works councils. The furthest the parties have been prepared to go on a consensual basis has been to incorporate a joint statement on the desirability of greater employee involvement in private-sector companies into the text of the Pro- gramme for Economic and Social Progress and the Programme for Competitiveness and Work. Meanwhile, progress on the ground has been slow.

Greater progress has been made in the public sector. This has re- flected less a strategic response to recent international business trends than thinking at European Community level on worker rights. In Ire- land the employee participation debate became more intense after entry into the European Community and resulted in much discussion and activity throughout the 1970s and early 1980s. The passing of the Worker Participation (State Enterprises) Act 1977 introduced board- level participation to seven semi-state companies and these provi- sions were extended to a number of other state organisations under the terms of the Worker Participation (State Enterprises) Act 1988. The 1988 Act also contained provisions for the establishment of sub- board participative structures, but allowed management and unions considerable leeway in tailoring forms of participation to the circum- stances of individual companies and agencies. The Act listed 39 semi-state companies and agencies as suited to introducing sub-board structures. By 1994, some 28 of these had established structures (Kelly and Hourihan, 1994). Much of the recent focus of the repre- sentative employee participation debate has again reflected develop- ments at European Union level where various policy documents have concentrated on board level participation, disclosure of financial information and participation through works councils.

Informed in part by industrial relations crises during 1993-94 in a number of semi-state companies and the competitive challenges now facing Irish business, the programme of the "Rainbow" Government of Fine Gael, Labour and Democratic Left, which assumed office in late 1994, contains a proposal to establish a unit in the department of Enterprise and Employment to foster management-union co-operation and employee participation. It remains to be seen whether this initiative will go the way of earlier units and initiatives in the same area or prove to be a more effective agent of change in industrial relations practice.

The Role of Trade Unions

The period from the early to the late 1980s witnessed the most serious and sustained decline in union membership and organisation in Ireland since the 1920s (Roche, 1994b). Over the past decade unions have faced something of a resurgence of employer opposition to recognition in small companies and more sophisticated union substitution strategies in a not inconsiderable number of multinational companies, particularly in the electronics sector (Roche, 1994b; Roche and Turner, 1994). A recent study of employee relations practices in newly established ("greenfield") companies found a high incidence of non-union firms (over 55 per cent) among new start-ups (Gunnigle, 1992; 1994). (Companies establishing greenfield plants and willing to concede union recognition now also seem more likely to insist on single-union recognition agreements.) The incidence of non-unionism in greenfield plants was mainly related to ownership and industrial sector. Indeed non-unionism was predominantly confined to US-owned firms. Most Irish, European and Japanese-owned companies recognised trade unions. The study also found that in the case of the great majority of new plants, the decision to pursue the non-union route was determined at corporate headquarters. This research points to the emergence of a vibrant non-union sector among greenfield manufacturing and service companies. It further appears likely that this trend will be accentuated by the increasing numbers and visibility of companies successfully pursuing the non-union route which, in turn, provide useful models for new organisations considering establishing on a non-union basis. Equally, the current industrial policy focus on high technology industries and internationally-traded services may reinforce growth in the non-union sector in the Republic of Ireland.

If this trend were to continue, as seems likely given the current thrust of industrial policy, the traditionally significant role of trade unions in manufacturing industry might conceivably be significantly eroded. It remains to be seen if these non-union companies will eventually concede recognition or succumb to unionisation in the face of persistent union organising efforts, ageing workforces, commercial problems, new trade union approaches to industrial relations, or an improved national economic climate and reduced unemployment levels. Moreover, there remains little solid evidence that new "human resource" strategies, involving innovations in work organisation, new forms of consultation and communication, and greater use of variable pay systems, in themselves critically affect either recognition or levels of organisation in private sector companies (see Roche and Turner, 1994). The fact that a number of well-known companies practise such policies as part of a policy of union avoidance or substitution cannot be taken to mean that in general companies implementing new industrial relations or human resource policies either wish to avoid or marginalise unions, or have succeeded in so doing. It might also be plausibly argued that the continuing legitimacy and acceptance of trade unions, as manifested both in the corporatist structures characteristic of Irish industrial relations and the traditional acceptance of trade unions as legitimate bargaining partners, creates a socio-economic climate conducive to ensuring the maintenance of high levels of trade union recognition and influence among new and established firms (see Roche and Turner, 1994).

For the foreseeable future unions will continue to play a pivotal role in Irish industrial relations and will have a major impact on the outcome of new industrial relations and human resource strategies. But intensified competitive pressures, new managerial strategies for industrial relations and the potential attractiveness to employers of marginalising unions or adopting the non-union option pose for Irish unions arguably their most serious strategic challenge since they became a pillar of Irish industrial relations in the first three decades after Independence.

The problems faced by unions in responding to the new agenda cannot be denied. Union officials and activists have been schooled, in the same way as Irish managers, in a tradition in which adversarial collective bargaining was viewed as the mainspring of industrial relations practice. Competing and meeting commercial challenges were viewed, first and foremost, as concerns of management. Co-operation with company efforts to increase employee commitment to business success is seen to hold risks of reduced commitment to the union. Though unions are being asked to assist with measures to enhance business performance, they must also be capable of challenging managerial decisions and negotiating pay and conditions in collective bargaining. New industrial relations strategies threaten to set in train a pervasive trend towards the decentralisation of industrial relations processes, possibly reducing the capacity of central trade union organisations to control developments at company level. Competitive pressures may lead in the short or long term to revisions in work organisation and pay regimes which, in the eyes of union members, involve serious disimprovements in working conditions. The expansion of atypical employment also poses problems for trade unions. Unions have long focused their recruiting and organising activities primarily on permanent workers. Recruiting and retaining part-time, temporary and contract workers poses greater difficulties. Representing atypical workers in individual and collective bargaining also poses major challenges. If multi-skilling, employee involvement and enhanced employment security for "core" workers may increasingly involve the parallel development of a "peripheral" workforce composed of atypical workers, unions may have to countenance the prospect of representing a dual workforce in companies. Not surprisingly, these latter features of the new industrial relations agenda are of particular concern to trade unions (see *IRN Report*, 1994, 4: 19).

To the degree, therefore, that unions openly endorse the new agenda of competitiveness, they may thus face particularly acute problems and dilemmas. The ICTU is also subject to such dilemmas of representation. This became clear during 1994 and 1995 when Congress was accused by some sections of membership of adopting an employers' agenda, or of doing the business of the State, when it sought to broker agreements in TEAM and Packard in circumstances of crisis and threatened closure. TQM and WCM may spark frictions or outright convulsions at the interface between different occupational categories and the unions that represent them. These difficulties and uncertainties have come to light in some of the major industrial relations crises of the late 1980s and early 1990s.

A significant aspect of the debate on employee participation in Ireland since the 1970s has concerned the role of trade unions. Traditionally the Irish trade union movement did not seem particularly committed to representative forms of employee participation such as worker directors or works councils (Morrissy, 1989). Reactions to participation through equity holding have been mixed and no discernible trend is evident. Indeed, apart from support for greater disclosure of information, the traditional trade union approach to employee participation has been marked by a considerable degree of apathy. Such apathy has strong links with the doubts many trade unionists harbour about the implications of representative participation for the union's role in collective bargaining.

In recent years Irish unions have begun to face up to and address these and related problems of representation under new industrial relations. The ICTU report, *New Forms of Work Organisation*, suggests that trade unions need to take a more proactive role in influencing the planning and implementation of the new management strategies. In the area of employee participation, the report encourages a particular focus on developing, and actively participating in, employee involvement initiatives at workplace level. This report also identifies key aspects of employee participation which trade unions need to address, particularly the joint monitoring of participation initiatives at workplace level, involvement of trade unions in the internal communications processes of organisations, access to and understanding of business information and involvement in high-level business decision-making.

Some of the major unions have also committed themselves to work "with the grain" of the new managerial agenda. Unions like SIPTU and the AEEU have held seminars and conferences on the implications of world class manufacturing and related techniques.

Unions have sought to enter and even foster "partnership" in a number of major companies. Some such companies, like ESB, Bord na Mona and Telecom (previously Posts and Telegraphs), had long provided textbook cases of adversarial industrial relations at their most highly developed.

In adopting this position unions are mindful, above all, that working with the new agenda appears the best, or the only, way of ensuring that Ireland responds to increased competitiveness by pursuing an industrial and labour market strategy based on high value-added, high skill and high wage employment. Edward Brown's and Peter Cassells' contributions to this book outline clearly the trade union rationale for doing business with new industrial relations and human resource policies and point to some of the dilemmas this will inevitably involve.

CONCLUSION

This chapter has sought to provide a context for the individual contributions to the book by highlighting the main challenges currently presented to the conduct of industrial relations in Ireland and the ways in which companies and trade unions have sought to respond. The scope and intensity of the debate currently under way in industrial relations may indicate a growing realisation on the part of the social partners, individually and collectively, that the adversarial model and its canons of good industrial relations were suited to a particular historical period of Irish economic and industrial development that has now all but passed. Given the transformation that is occurring in international economic conditions, it seems to be increasingly accepted that the adversarial model no longer provides a viable basis for relations between employees, unions and employers in Ireland.

PART ONE

THE MANAGEMENT OF CHANGE

2

Industrial Relations and Adjustment at the Level of the Enterprise

Alfred Pankert
International Labour Organisation, Geneva

The management of change at the level of the enterprise is certainly very topical. Many enterprises today have to go through adjustment processes — sometimes rather dramatic ones — in order to remain competitive in the face of an ever-increasing globalisation of markets. These adjustment processes are of various types, but the most important ones — which are often closely linked to each other — are the introduction of new forms of work organisations, the introduction of new technologies or the very restructuring of the enterprise.

The purpose of this paper is to introduce a discussion on the relationship between industrial relations and adjustment at the level of the enterprise. My main point will be that industrial relations can make a very significant — and probably irreplaceable — contribution to enterprise adjustment, but only if the parties have been able to devise procedures and practices which are sufficiently well adapted to the problems to be dealt with.

As an International Labour Office (ILO) official I am not going to approach the subject — and would actually not be able to approach it — by providing you with detailed information on the specific adjustment experiences of one or several enterprises. Instead, I shall try in the first place to offer a few general comments, from an ILO perspective, on how to approach the issue of enterprise adjustment, and in the second place to give a brief overview of the global situation prevailing at present in industrial market economies.

In recent years, an ever-increasing emphasis has been placed in industrial market economies on the fact that labour-management cooperation is extremely important, and probably indispensable, for the successful adjustment of enterprises. I should like to make two general observations in this respect.

The first is that the increasing emphasis on the need for labour-management co-operation should not hide the fact that there is not — and that there never will be — a complete identity of interests between employers and workers. There can be no doubt that both employers and workers have a long-term common interest in the successful operation of the enterprise and that anything to be distributed must first be produced. But this does not exclude that there are also divergent interests between the parties, particularly in the short and medium term. The most obvious examples are those of the level of wages and of employment security. For the workers, good wages and effective protection against dismissal are essential factors for the maintenance of a decent life. For the employers, on the contrary, wages represent a production cost which weakens the competitive position of the enterprise. Similarly, any limitation of the right to terminate the employment of workers restricts the scope of management prerogatives as well as the adaptability of the enterprise. It would therefore be unrealistic to assume that the interests of employers and workers are fundamentally convergent or to base a call for systematic labour-management co-operation on such an assumption.

It should be recognised that employers and workers can have divergent interests and that the real issue is to find ways and means to reconcile those interests. The purpose of industrial relations is precisely to reconcile divergent interests through compromises which are the result of a give-and-take process between the parties. We shall see later that this will always be achieved through some form of collective bargaining or workers' participation, but that the concrete way in which it will be achieved will vary according to countries, branches of activity and enterprises.

My second general observation is that, in the particular instance of enterprise adjustment, the purpose of the compromise to be sought by the parties should be, on the one hand, to allow the effective introduction of the changes which are needed to maintain the competitiveness for the enterprise and, on the other hand, to give a social dimension to the adjustment process, i.e. to minimise its negative effects and to maximise its positive effects for the workforce, both in quantitative and in qualitative terms.

Why should the adjustment process have a social dimension? There are two main reasons for this. The first, which is of a rather philosophical nature, is that economic development should not be an end in itself. Although this is a very important issue, I am not going to dwell on it, because I assume that everybody basically agrees with it. The second reason, which I shall develop somewhat more, is that adjustment will stand many more chances of being successful if it has a social dimension. The adjustment process will normally not be effective if it takes the short-sighted approach which is almost exclusively directed at cutting costs and, more particularly, labour costs. Those who follow this path risk taking what has sometimes been called the "low road" and locking themselves into the vicious circle of low wages, low skills, low quality jobs and low productivity.

Adjustment is likely to be much more successful if one takes the long-term approach which aims at genuinely increasing the adaptive and innovative capacity of the enterprise. This objective can hardly be achieved without a well-qualified workforce and without a well-motivated workforce in terms of wages, working conditions and job satisfaction. That is exactly what is meant when one speaks about the social dimension of the adjustment process. Giving such a dimension to the adjustment process is completely in line with the increasingly held conviction that human resources are nowadays by far the most important asset for economic success.

The necessity to give a social dimension to the adjustment process, and the role which industrial relations can play to this end, is not mere theory. One can indeed refer to a number of instances where well functioning industrial relations systems have been instrumental in giving a social dimension to economic development generally, and to various adjustment processes in particular, and where this has, in turn, contributed to good economic performance generally, and to successful adjustment in particular. One must of course admit that such contributions cannot be scientifically measured, mainly because there are at least as may qualitative aspects to the issue as there are quantitative ones. Moreover, good economic performance and successful adjustment are always due to a number of reasons rather than to one single reason. It can nevertheless be noted that two top economic performers, the former Federal Republic of Germany and Japan, both have a well developed system of collective bargaining; that the former Federal Republic of Germany has, in addition, a highly developed labour legislation and the most advanced system of workers' participation of the western world; and that Japan has, besides its collective bargaining system, a system of joint consultation which works exceptionally well.

Referring more particularly to adjustment, there are studies which suggest that adjustment programmes in which the workers have been involved, and which have consequently had a social dimension, have been more effective than those which have followed a mere cost-cutting approach. Several studies show, for example, that in the United States rubber tyre industry and in certain parts of the British furniture industry, where adjustment programmes mainly based on cuts in wages and other labour costs had been carried out in the late 1970s and the early 1980s, many factories have nevertheless had to close down shortly after the cuts had been made. Another study shows that the Swedish shipbuilding sector has, on the contrary, successfully achieved a major restructuring in the late 1970s and the early 1980s and attributes this success, at least in part, to the fact that the whole process had taken place within a tripartite framework, involving the concerned efforts of employers, trade unions and national and local governments. In the former Federal Republic of Germany, the coal mining sector — which has, together with the steel sector, the most advanced co-determination system in the western world — was able to implement a drastic adjustment programme without major problems. Other examples suggesting similar conclusions could be given as well.

I should like to emphasise very strongly, however, that I do not advocate the transplantation of the Swedish, the Japanese or — even less — the German system to any other country. As is amply known, each industrial relations system has developed in a specific context and can only work effectively in that context. The few examples I have given do, nevertheless, strongly suggest — and this is the point I want to make — that good economic performance and successful adjustment are not made more difficult, indeed they are less difficult, if they are supported by a well developed and well functioning industrial relations system.

It is probably the increasing awareness of the potentially positive influence of good industrial relations on economic performance and adjustment which prompted President Clinton to set up recently a Commission which includes several former Secretaries of Labour as well as a number of eminent representatives from employers', workers' and academic circles to "investigate the current state of labour-management relations and labour law and make recommendations concerning changes that may be needed to improve productivity through increased worker-management co-operation and employee participation in the workplace". This initiative seems particularly noteworthy, both because industrial relations have been playing an ever-decreasing role in the United States in recent years and because the creation of national commissions to deal with industrial relations issues has always been exceptional in that country.

I should now like to address the way in which industrial relations are contributing to enterprise adjustment in industrial market economies, that is, about the types of relations which are used for that purpose and about the main obstacles which must be overcome for these types of relations to work effectively.

There are basically two forms of industrial relations: collective bargaining and workers' participation in decisions. Workers' participation is often referred to as "institutional participation" and as "direct participation".

The term "institutional participation" refers to workers participating in decisions through elected representatives who sit on certain institutions. The most common form of such participation is that which takes place through works councils or similar joint consultation bodies. In certain countries, such as Germany or the Scandinavian countries, the arrangements for institutional participation are quite formal because they are based on detailed legislative or contractual provisions. In other countries, such as the United Kingdom, they are based on more or less informal understanding between the parties.

The term "direct participation" refers to workers being called upon to participate directly in the decisions concerning the execution of their daily work. Examples would be the various forms of autonomous work groups or quality circles. Although these forms of participation do not by themselves involve the intervention of any representatives of the workers, there are some instances where management has negotiated with the trade unions or with the works council the general conditions under which such forms of participation may be introduced and implemented. It must, however, be added that such instances seem to be rare.

Which of these various forms of industrial relations can most effectively contribute to enterprise adjustment? This depends, of course, on what one wants to achieve. If the objective is to actively involve all workers in the decisions concerning their daily work, an appropriate form of direct participation is required which cannot be achieved — at least not exclusively — through collective bargaining or institutional participation. In all other cases, adjustment measures can be designed and implemented through collective bargaining or institutional participation, that is, through an understanding reached between management and a representation of the workers in a collective agreement or during a discussion in a works council or a similar joint consultation body.

The question then arises whether collective bargaining and institutional participation are interchangeable forms of industrial relations for those forms of adjustment which do not require any form of direct participation. Basically, the answer to this question is in the affirmative. It can indeed be noted that in countries such as the United States, where institutional participation has traditionally played an insignificant role, enterprise adjustment has essentially been implemented through collective bargaining. It would seem, however, that institutional participation is a more appropriate instrument for enterprise adjustment. Although it is not always easy to draw a sharp distinction between collective bargaining and institutional participation, international experience shows that collective bargaining is mainly used to deal, on a *periodic* basis, with a *limited* number of issues, such as wages and hours, which are of a rather conflictual nature.

Institutional participation, on the contrary, is mainly used to deal — on a more *permanent* basis and in a more *co-operative* spirit — with a relatively broad range of issues, such as those which concern the various aspects of work organisation. This seems to imply that the enterprises which do not yet have a permanent and well functioning joint consultation system would have a clear interest in developing one. If it is true that the traditional forms of collective bargaining can make a significant contribution to effective enterprise adjustment, and that collective bargaining can even be the most appropriate means for establishing the general framework and the basic parameters for certain types of adjustment processes, it is equally true that the vast majority of the issues arising in the course of enterprise adjustment can be dealt with most effectively through an appropriate joint consultation machinery.

Over the last 10 to 15 years important developments have been taking place, although to varying degrees, in many industrial market economies as regards the forms of industrial relations most commonly used to deal with adjustment problems. The main features are, on the one hand, the increasing recourse to informal types of joint consultation and, on the other hand, the increasing recourse to various forms of direct participation. The new types of joint consultation frequently lack any legal or contractual basis, take place outside any formal body and are not regulated by any formal procedure. In a number of instances, the new forms of joint consultation co-exist with more formal ones which were established earlier and which tend to lose ground with the passage of time.

The new forms of direct participation generally entail an integration of the conception, the execution and the control of work. The ensuing redesign of work normally supposes a drastic simplification of the job classification system, multiple-skilling of workers and, by way of consequence, improved and broader vocational training.

The increasing recourse to informal joint consultation and to direct participation is frequently the result of management initiatives. The growing use of these forms of industrial relations is essentially a response to the perceived need of management for greater flexibility in order to ensure the competitiveness of the enterprise. The fact that new forms of industrial relations are emerging or expanding in response to changing needs is in itself a sound development which can only be welcomed — provided, however, that the legitimate interests of the workers are safeguarded.

It is precisely in this regard that the increasing recourse to informal joint consultation and to direct participation is giving rise to concern. Attempts are being made in a number of instances to avoid the involvement of trade unions in the design and implementation of the new arrangements. Sometimes a works council or similar body is involved, but often even these bodies are circumvented in an attempt to deal directly with the workers themselves. Where this is the case, there is actually a shift of certain issues from the domain of collective relations to that of individual relations, and sometimes even a shift from "industrial relations", which is a bilateral decision-making process, to "human resources management", which is essentially a unilateral decision-making process. These trends are quite strong in certain countries such as the United Kingdom and, more particularly, the United States. They are clearly less pronounced in the countries of continental Europe, but are nevertheless giving rise to some concern there too.

To be fair, it must be added that these developments have sometimes been encouraged — or, at least been made easier — by the fact that in the late 1970s and the early 1980s many trade unions have been slow to recognise the need for more flexible forms of industrial relations and, more generally, the need for rapid adjustment to a drastically changing environment. Whatever the situation may be in this regard, it would seem that one of the most important problems in the years to come will be to devise practices which are sufficiently flexible to ensure effective enterprise adjustment and which ensure, at the same time, the active involvement of a collective representation of the workers, that is, the trade union and/or a representation of the works council type. The need for such a collective representation seems indispensable, at least in the medium and long term, if major imbalances are to be avoided. Experience shows very clearly that a system of checks and balances is indispensable, not only in the political sphere but also in the economic and social spheres, if basic values such as democracy and social equity are to be safeguarded.

The search for formulas ensuring both sufficient flexibility of the adjustment process and sufficient involvement of a collective representation of the workers in this process is probably the most crucial problem in the field of enterprise adjustment at the present time. There are, however, other problems, including ones concerning the contents and scope of labour-management relations regarding enterprise adjustment. A major difficulty concerns the delimitation of the issues which should be considered as management prerogatives and of those which should be dealt with jointly by management and labour. It is well known that the delimitation between these two types of issues can differ according to countries and that it can change over time.

The current practice in industrial market economies is that decisions on the very principle and basic nature of adjustment are taken by management, and that the modalities of adjustment are discussed jointly by management and labour with the objective of minimising the negative and maximising the positive consequences for the workers. As will be seen later, these discussions are generally of a consultative nature. Since the domain of management prerogatives has never been defined once and for all, it is clear that the workers are entitled to challenge the existing practice at any time. The experience of a number of countries shows, however, that many difficulties are created, with no profit for anybody, if the current practice is systematically challenged by the workers — even at a time when no change of that practice can reasonably be expected because the time is obviously not ripe for such a change. Experience also seems to show that it is better to deal with the problem of the extent of management prerogatives at the central level in order to promote uniform practices throughout the country, rather than letting each branch of activity of each enterprise work out its own solution.

Other major difficulties are bound to arise in the course of labour-management dealings on adjustment if the parties do not agree on the meaning of the concept of consultation. The workers quickly lose interest in consultation if management considers it as a pure formality, that is, if the decisions of management are actually taken before consultation starts and are not influenced by it. Employers will perhaps object that consultation, unlike negotiation and co-determination, does not limit the right of management to take the final decision. This is undoubtedly correct from the legal point of view. It remains true, nevertheless, that workers are not really interested in consultation unless the employers agree to enter into genuine discussions with them whenever there is a divergence of opinion. There is probably no solution to this problem which can fully satisfy a sharp-minded lawyer.

The best advice one can give is probably that the principle of the non-binding nature of consultation may not be challenged at the level of the principles, but that one should accept at the same time that consultation can in fact come rather close to negotiation. It should also be added, however, that if consultation is taken seriously by management, and if the workers are really involved in the decision-making process, they should also feel responsible for the implementation of the decisions which have been taken. The effective functioning of all forms of workers' participation is subject to a number of conditions, and the most essential include the need not only for a genuine sharing in the taking of decisions, but also for a genuine sharing in the responsibility for implementing them.

Finally, I should like to point out that labour management dealings on adjustment issues at the enterprise level will normally be easier if they are embedded in a context of well-functioning industrial relations at all levels. This supposes, for example, effective channels of communication between employers' and workers' organisations at the level of the branch of activity and at the central level, effective labour disputes settlement procedures at all levels and, most importantly perhaps, a fundamentally positive attitude of employers and workers towards each other and the firm belief by on both sides in the virtues of social dialogue. This means, in other words, that enterprise adjustment stands the best chance of being successful if there is a genuine industrial relations "culture". It is obvious that long and patient efforts are required of all industrial relations parties in order to build up such a culture.

3

Trade Unions and the Management of Change

Edmund Browne
Joint General President,
Services Industrial Professional Technical Union

The university of life teaches that change is an inexorable companion through the journey of life. Who would argue? We have all known the pain and the pleasure.

"What is the stars?", Joxer wondered with awesome incredulity. "What is change?" we might ask with equal wonderment. Change is constant — slow, even imperceptible at times, otherwise fast like a falling comet, sometimes enhancing, sometimes degrading.

The global village has been introduced as the product of monumental change. In the economy of the global village internationally mobile capital coexists happily with extreme human degradation, suffering and exploitation on the one hand, and extreme manifestations of wealth on the other. Barriers to the realisation of the global village were undoubtedly removed with the overnight collapse of the Soviet bloc. But at the same time, new tensions have appeared as the people of central and eastern Europe also appreciate more clearly the gulf between wealth and poverty that accompanies the free market.

Within this global context, the Irish economic and social microcosm has exhibited similar characteristics of unfairness, injustice, greed and cruelty — though to an admittedly muted degree.

In the decades since the 1960s Ireland has been transformed socially, economically and industrially and there is even evidence of political change. The trade union movement has played its part in this transformation but there remains a great deal more to be achieved before we can say that we have a just and caring society.

In that struggle the commitment to solidarity between all workers, both nationally and internationally, must never be diminished. That ideal significantly inspired the two programmes which sought balanced social and economic development. The Programme for National Recovery (PNR) and Programme for Economic and Social Progress (PESP) witnessed steady if modest real progress in incomes, loosened the grip of poverty on those blighted by low pay and social welfare, and advanced other trade union priorities. The business climate was transformed by vast improvements in productivity, unit labour costs and competitiveness. The big failure was, of course, the demoralising and apparently uncontrollable spiral of unemployment.

Unemployment cannot be explained simplistically, however tempting it may be to do so. Of the factors contributing we can identify:

- inadequate job creation
- the failure of the private sector to implement its job creating commitments
- international recession
- demographic pressures
- structural change
- declining emigration/migration
- the job destructive capacity of technological innovation
- job destruction in the public sector
- rationalisation and re-organisation
- growing competition for international mobile investment
- dismantling of the constraining/humanising social parameters to economic development — nationally, regionally and internationally
- the forces of international competition facilitated by the huge gaps in labour costs and social and living conditions
- failures in the market place due to bad management or misguided corporate strategies
- the development of regional economic integrated markets without regard to balanced social infrastructure creating free-fire zones for transnational corporations in the context of wages and social values.

So far I have been attempting to describe the economic and social conditions, both nationally and internationally, which have profoundly accelerated the pace and determined the nature of change. The same factors compel a re-examination of the way in which the world of manufacturing is managed and provoke consideration of the concept of equal partnership of progress with solidarity at enterprise level — including an agreed and transparent focus on the fundamentals which

determine the success or failure of the enterprise, including a comprehensive social dimension within the enterprise — and an acceptance
of the equal status of labour in the participative and informed control
of the enterprise.

What is change? Indeed, this question has been exercising the
minds of trade unionists across the western world for some time now.
The Irish Congress of Trade Unions (ICTU) has commissioned an examination of change in work organisation and the management of
human resources and the resulting report is of profound importance
for enterprise/workers alike. The report has identified trade union response options which are at an early stage of consideration but which,
I believe, will shape the future of industrial relations in this country.

Meantime, the Services Industrial Professional and Technical Union (SIPTU) has been there and is well advanced with a programme to
introduce and inform officials and shop stewards of the "dark secrets"
of Total Quality Management, including its positive and negative potential for workers, for trade unions and for enterprises and, perhaps
most importantly, stimulating the debate about the appropriate trade
union response.

Let's examine some options:

1. *The What-We-Have-We-Hold Option.* Under this option trade unions would oppose the introduction of any work organisation initiatives which disturb the current status quo. Accordingly, they
   would refuse to co-operate with teamwork, total quality management, JIT etc. Members would be instructed not to co-operate with
   management who tried to introduce these concepts.

2. *The Suck-It-and-See Option.* Rather than taking a formal policy
   stance on the question of co-operation with new work organisation
   initiatives, trade unions could allow local officials and shop stewards to decide on a case by case basis. The decision on whether or
   not to co-operate would be made individually "on the ground" by
   the personnel involved, without referral to the central trade union.

3. *The Reactive Approach Option.* The assumption underlying this
   option is that trade unions, given certain assurances, will co-
   operate with the introduction of new work organisation initiatives.
   In response to management initiatives, trade unions would develop
   clear policies and provide specific guidelines to their officials on
   what initiatives should be co-operated with and under what terms.

These guidelines would provide a "floor" below which unions would not be prepared to go.

4. *The Proactive Approach Option.* Under this option it is assumed that trade unions believe that the introduction of work organisation initiatives will, on balance, be of benefit to their members. In order to ensure the best interests of their members are served it is important that trade unions are seen to respond positively and have as much input as possible into the decisions about the introduction as well as the ongoing monitoring of the initiatives.

5. *The State-of-the-Art Approach Option.* This would involve trade unions in actively promoting the introduction of work organisation initiatives within companies. This would arise where the trade unions believed that the introduction of these new approaches would be in the best long term interests of the members. In order to ensure that trade unions were closely involved, they would actively promote their introduction in companies. Opportunities could also arise in situations where companies were in crisis and required a radically new approach to ensure their survival.

The benefits and risks of these options can be summarised as follows:

1. *The What-We-Have-We-Hold Option*
Benefits:
* Maintains traditional adversarial approach
* No need for union to adapt or change
Risks:
* Unions by-passed by management
* Members questioning relevance and value of union membership
* Miss opportunity to be involved in QWL programmes
* Damage to Ireland's perception

2. *The Suck It-and-See Option*
Benefits:
* Allows issues to be addressed without having a formal policy
* Maintains adversarial position nationally, while presenting a "positive" response locally.
* No blurring of traditional industrial relations agenda
* No need for unions to change or adapt

Risks:

- Wide variety of local practices
- No support or guidance from trade unions
- Reacting rather than influencing management proposals
- QWL initiative with management

3. *The Reactive Approach Option*
Benefits:

- Provides clear policy and guidelines
- Provides framework for local officials and members
- Maintains uniformity of approach

Risks:

- Takes no account of
  — local practices
  — existing relationships
  — reasons for and scope of initiatives
- Limits scope of local officials to develop optimum solution
- Could be perceived as negative, if conditional upon achieving "up-front" agreement.

4. *The Proactive Approach Option*
Benefits:

- Allows for a tailor made approach
- Allows unions to optimise their level of input
- Opportunity for greater involvement of members
- Builds member identification with union
- More involved in shaping final outcomes

Risks:

- Could blur traditional "us and them" relationships
- Blurring of traditional bargaining agenda
- Undermining of union solidarity
- Variety of local outcomes

5. *The State-of-the-Art Approach Option*
Benefits:

- More involved in setting the agenda
- Seen to address wider member needs
- Closely involved in ongoing monitoring

Risks:

- Could be perceived as "doing management's job"
- Undermining of union solidarity

The case has yet to be fully debated and considered.

This is by no means an Irish problem. Indeed, Total Quality Management and other state-of-the-art management strategies/techniques mostly originate in Japan and find their way here within the American multinationals. What is abundantly clear is that the traditional management approach is essentially history. In its place is emerging the multi-faceted but coherent series of management initiatives labelled Total Quality Management/World Class Manufacturing and designed to achieve:

- employee loyalty
- customer orientation
- quality
- continuous improvement
- partnership

These new forms of management, enterprise structure and work organisation are industry's response to intense global competition, technological change and smart workers. Key concepts include:

- communicating management
- by-passing unions
- customer is king
- flexible workforce
- smart working employees
- delayered management
- new and flexible reward systems

A trade union response which goes beyond outright opposition will emphasise the following trade union priorities:

1. The need to extend employee involvement above the levels of work process and production problem-solving to areas of business strategy and company finance. Unless this is done efforts to establish employee involvement at the process level are unlikely to be sustainable in the medium term.

2. The need to ensure that the search for flexibility through team working, job rotation and multi-skilling is carried through in the context of improving the quality of working life and work force skills. Otherwise, in time, it will be seen as simply an attempt by management "to get more for less" and to de-skill some groups in

the workforce while providing others with minimum additional skills.

3. The need to ensure that legitimate efforts to be customer responsive and to reduce lead times do not lead to excessive stress and pressure on the workforce. This would imply that "full development", "just in time" production may not be possible and that some buffer stocks would still be produced.

4. The need to ensure that supplier companies and their work forces are not reduced to a second class dependence status by more powerful core companies.

Some of the trade union response options depend on high quality industrial relationships which are characterised by trust between union, employee and management which is far from being a universal feature of the Irish industrial relations scene. Indeed, industrial relations experience in Ireland covers the complete spectrum from chronic confrontation to benign co-operation.

For example, a small number of current disputes expose the ugly face of the ruthless exploitative employer, reviving memories of some of the worst excesses of "Murphyism" in the first decade of the twentieth century. The efforts of some companies to deny workers' trade union rights, constitutionally guaranteed, and supported by the Labour Relations Commission, require a major solidarity response from trade unionists everywhere and should be equally condemned and rejected by all fair-mined employers.

These and other legitimate trade disputes in defence of workers' rights raise serious questions about the Industrial Relations Act of 1990 which has been demonstrated as supportive of those employers who seek to crush the spirit of workers. In a fair society, labour legislation must uphold and support the rights of workers and sustain the rulings of the Labour Relations Commission and the Labour Court on issues concerning workers' rights to join trade unions. I believe the Industrial Relations Act of 1990 must be urgently reformed to embrace these basic ideals. Without losing sight of the diversity of industrial relations experience it seems clear to me that the trade union response should embrace the state-of-the-art option described above.

There can be no doubting the totality of our need to seek to maximise the employment creation potential within existing industry and to subscribe positively and constructively to the creation of a social and economic environment which will enable "Ireland Incorporated" to compete successfully with internationally mobile investment and to facilitate the development of indigenous industry. I am deeply conscious of the fact that Ireland is a low-wage economy by comparison with the wealthier nations, and I am fully aware that to secure a growth in living standards for more of our people in Irish circumstances requires that we be extremely pro-active in the areas of productivity, quality and competitiveness.

The state-of-the-art option would place the trade union movement at the cutting edge of progress, enabling the union to go on the offensive in terms of setting the agenda for progressive change and development. Indeed, I believe that the failure of the PESP in the area of job creation is significantly due to the fact that employment-related issues of a positive nature have not been on the agenda traditionally shared by management and unions at enterprise level.

Such radical innovation on behalf of the trade union movement would, of course, require a massive culture change — mostly, I believe, on the part of managers. In this respect I should point out that the historical relationships between unions and employers essentially have been driven by management, firstly in its embrace of what is described as the Fordism principles of mass production, which historically relegated workers to being appendages of the machine in mass production, and then in the discovery by management that workers have brains — a discovery that underpins the development of world class manufacturing and total quality management.

Naturally, many workers will react defensively, as will trade unions, to the considerable changes inherent in these new techniques and concepts. However, I believe that the trade union movement should adjust and adapt, not only to accommodate this new environment, but to exploit in a constructive manner the opportunities which it presents to enhance the quality of life in the workplace, to seek to achieve new plateau's of responsibility and reward within the workplace, and to determine the relationship based on equal partnership and equalitive participation.

There is, of course, the transitional corporation dimension. The transnational corporation is a creature of the global village of which Ireland is but a mere suburb — thus the successful implementation of the ultimate trade union response to Total Quality Management necessarily involves international relationships. We must, therefore, recognise the importance of trade union solidarity across national borders and the development of European Works Councils with the European Community (EC) Social Charter to facilitate this necessary development. Similarly, given the nature of the transnational corporation the new agenda increasingly must focus on international comparisons in respect of pay and conditions, the status of the local enterprise in terms of productivity, competitiveness and quality, and the sometimes uncompromising dictates of the market places. Some of these determinants are already very much in place — for example, many enterprises are obliged by international pressures to adopt the ISO 9000 series of quality standards as a precondition for successful activity in the market place. This, of course, has major implications and must increasingly become a focus of the industrial relations environment.

In the natural order of things, the diversity of the industrial relations experience will dictate the trade union response and this is as it should be. The state-of-the-art option requires a very high level of trust in industrial relations which requires that trade unions be accepted by management as something more meaningful than an irritating outside presence. Whilst SIPTU has established and sustained excellent relationships with many workers and the enterprise, there are all too frequently employers who seek to marginalise the union, including some who are acclaimed for the quality of their approach to human relationships within the enterprise. All too frequently in recent experience it is "macho" arbitrary management which creates industrial unrest and all too frequently, too, companies which are welcome guests of the nation indulge in various sophisticated methods to cut off workers from their natural trade union relations. Such short-sighted policies tend, over time, to generate a "them and us" environment which is exactly what SIPTU seeks to avoid in cultivating the legitimate social and economic aspirations of Irish workers.

4

Strategy Formulation and Implementation in a Context of Change

Sarah Moore

*Department of Personnel and
Employment Relations, University of Limerick*

INTRODUCTION

This paper sets out some of the central issues that arise in managing change in today's business environment and presents a conceptual model which has as its aim the provision of effective guidelines for the management of strategic change. A brief discussion of the current business environment is presented, with a focus on the role that industrial relations and personnel management can play in the successful management of change.

CHANGE IN TODAY'S BUSINESS ENVIRONMENT

The increasing rapidity with which change is occurring in all business environments has been well documented over the past 20 years. Major upheavals have occurred in the practices, procedures and strategic focus of very many companies, to the extent that an increasing number of variables need to be understood and integrated into any change programme. Trends in management and industrial relations have seen efforts to redirect a focus from competition to one of co-operation between management and employees. The range of forces which have emerged include fundamental economic aspects such as global competition, deregulation, new technology and, increasingly, changing workforce demographics (Thompson, 1991). Traditional methods of managing and responding to work processes have become less relevant in environments which are now more dynamic, more competitive and potentially more threatening than ever before.

The wider context of organisational change has been recognised as a key challenge to all businesses, particularly due to the structural, political and psychological difficulties associated with ongoing change programmes (Toffler, 1971, 1980; Naisbitt, 1980; Handy, 1990). Handy argues that we can no longer use the concept of "continuous [stable and relatively predictable] change" as our framework for understanding and managing organisational progress, but rather, changes are now much more likely to be "discontinuous" in the sense that they do not form part of a predictable pattern and require constant flexibility. Traditional processes for dealing with all business activity, both internal and external, can no longer be relied upon:

> We are entering an Age of Unreason, where in so many ways the future is there to be shaped by us and for us; a time when the only prediction that will hold true is that no predictions will hold true (Handy, 1990: 4).

If change is as radical and as unprecedented as theorists such as Handy would claim, the questions remains: how can this change be managed?

There is such a varied array of literature and evidence relating to the management of change that it is legitimate to question how any one approach can be seen as workable or appropriate. The search for a unifying model for tackling change is as yet unresolved. Recent literature would suggest that it is naive to limit the horizons of strategic change management by being "prematurely paradigmatic" (Daft and Buenger, 1990), and that the development of a model for strategy and change is simply not possible. However, there is also a strong belief that due to the decreasing levels of predictability in practically all business environments there is a greater need than ever before to develop meaningful models which incorporate the diversity of thought and perspectives necessary for the management of change (e.g. Ansoff, 1987).

This paper includes a brief examination of a model of strategic management developed by the author in order to clarify the elements of strategic change which need to be considered, to provide guidelines for focusing on important strategic links and to illustrate the potential for a wider involvement in change from all areas in the organisation.

THE ROLE OF INDUSTRIAL RELATIONS AND PERSONNEL MANAGEMENT ISSUES

With the various demands and pressures relating to change, the relevance of industrial relations and personnel management issues must no longer be underestimated. For too long, industrial relations practitioners have been charged with the responsibility for dealing with the *effects* of strategic change without having an input into the formulation and planning of such change. This tendency is inevitably problematic. It has long been argued that unless different organisational groups participate in the planning of change, it may ultimately be much more difficult to bring that change about. For example, commitment and involvement are seen as being central to any successful attempt to bring about change, and such commitment must be obtained from every part of the organisation required to carry out the activities leading to change (Guth and MacMillan, 1989). It has been suggested that organisation-wide involvement in strategic change may have a very significant and positive effect on performance, particularly due to the increasing need for good quality information derived from a wide variety of sources inside the organisation (Hussey, 1991). This suggestion is supported by research carried out by Woolridge and Floyd (1990), who suggest that there are significant links between involvement with strategic change and organisational performance, not only because of the possibility of increased commitment, but also due to the wider range of information which is made available.

Recent literature has promoted the idea that there are benefits to be gained from integrating industrial relations and personnel management functions into the overall strategic change processes of the organisation (e.g. Fombrun, 1986; Schuler and Jackson, 1987). Such claims have been supported by commonly held views within Irish Industry. A representative view, derived from a series of qualitative interviews carried out by the author, is summed up in the following quote:

> "Throughout our entire change process, the management of industrial relations is seen to have played a vital part in the company's turnaround. This is particularly important in the light of increasing productivity needs where mechanisation, job redesign and the development of multiskilling are now being implemented in order to achieve the survival goals of the organisation. Unless industrial relations issues had been managed from the outset, with the relevant people involved, much of these interventions would have literally been impossible" (CEO of an Irish manufacturing company).

The message seems to be that as the challenge for change becomes more immediate and more intense, the clear divisions of responsibility between formulating plans for change and implementing them become considerably blurred. People who are affected by the change need to be active participants of the change programme, rather than passive reactors to change agendas set by others.

A Model for the Management of Strategic Change

The following model has been constructed using a combination of a review of contemporary literature on strategic change, and in-depth qualitative interviews with top management teams in Irish organisations. One way to consolidate the various linkages between the elements of strategic change is through the development of coherent strategic models as shown below:

A FRAMEWORK FOR DECISION-MAKING ANALYSIS

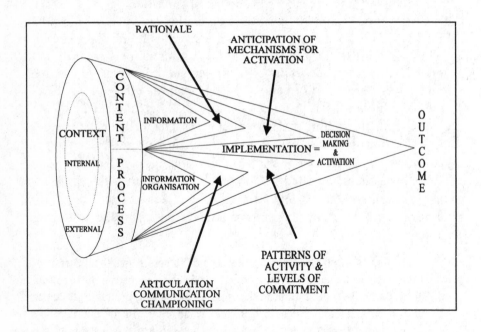

The three central variables contained in the model are outlined below:

1. *The context of the change*: i.e. any external contextual factors which are likely to have an impact on the business and how it operates or any internal or contextual component which has the potential to set the scene for changes in the organisation. When examining context in relation to change, the most relevant question is "Why is the strategy for change being pursued, given the contextual pressures, constraints and opportunities that exist".

External contextual factors include: Geographical location; political conditions; government regulations; economic factors; client profiles; supplier relationships; culture; competitors; and public pressure groups.

Internal contextual factors include: Managerial structure; internal corporate culture; internal political conditions; union activity; resource availability; and frameworks of strategic alliances.

Before change can be planned successfully, a detailed analysis of the context of the organisation should be carried out in order to reveal key aspects of both the internal and external settings and their relationships with each other. Much has been written about the need to match the organisation's internal context with its external context. For example, if an external environment is characterised by a lack of predictability and constant change, the internal context should be structured accordingly by having flexible structures and an adaptable culture (Mintzberg 1980).

2. *The content of the change*: i.e. the information and action items contained in the plan for change. When examining the content of any strategy for change, the most relevant questions are: "What is the strategy for change being pursued, using what information, derived from where and based on what business rationale?"

Before a given plan for change is decided upon, it is important to examine the information which has been used. The following represent guidelines for the critical examination of the content of change:

- Has there been an adequate search for, and use of, relevant information? Are there any gaps in the information search?

- Is the rationale for change based on correct assumptions, and if not, should there be a further investigation into the information currently being used?

- Is there sufficient anticipation of "mechanisms for activation"? No matter how good the rationale for change actually is, it is useless unless it can be implemented, so the content of any plan should consider how this will happen.

3. *The change process*: i.e. the ways in which the change is formulated and implemented in order to reach the desired outcome. When examining the change process it is important to focus on how the

change is being implemented; how the information is organised; how the plan is articulated, communicated and championed; the ways in which patterns of activity are emerging and the levels of commitment that exist.

> Organisations which successfully manage change are those which have integrated their human resource management policies with their strategies and the strategic change process (Johnson and Scholes, 1993: 416).

The process of change is often the element of strategy which tends to receive the least consideration. Yet it is this element which appears to be the most problematic aspect of achieving successful change. Alexander (1986) has identified common problems in dealing with process issues relating to change. These include: time factors, the surfacing of unexpected threats; co-ordination errors; insufficient commitment; resistance to change; inadequate leadership and the unclear definition of tasks. Unless such potential problems are recognised the time and effort which has been devoted to the change programme may be lost. For this reason, process issues need to be considered from the outset of any plan for change and must be considered in the same detail as the other two elements.

The recognition and integration of all the variables contained in the above model is not an easy task. It is this author's contention that such a task can be considerably facilitated by increased involvement from different alliances and levels within the organisation. The model presented is designed as a general guide for the analysis and improvement of strategic change management. A further aim is to present strategic change as a highly dynamic and iterative process, requiring constant re-evaluation and reformulation. While any change programme needs to move forward efficiently, there should also be room for manoeuvre to previous stages of the change in order to continue to test its effectiveness in an often rapidly changing business environment. The ability of an organisation to be simultaneously aware of context, content and process issues represents one of the keys to the successful management of change.

5

Current Themes in Organisational Design and Work Restructuring

Michael Morley

*Department of Personnel and
Employment Relations, University of Limerick*

INTRODUCTION

There is a quiet revolution taking place in many organisations. The source of the revolution, according to Block (1992), is the growing realisation that strict tight controls, greater work pressure, more clearly defined jobs, and tighter supervision have, in the last 50 years, run their course in terms of their ability to give organisations the productivity gains required to compete effectively. Attention is shifting to the need for employees personally to take responsibility for the success of businesses if organisations hope to survive and prosper.

The strategic imperative of the 1990s (Buchanan and McCalman, 1989) has heightened the argument for a more comprehensive approach to organisational design and work structuring, and set it within a new macro context defined by developments in labour markets, product markets, trading conditions and manufacturing technology. As Hoerr et al (1986) point out:

> The solution to fading competitive ability, sluggish productivity growth and poor quality cannot be found in the mythical black box of a miraculous technology. To realise ... full potential ... leading edge companies are integrating workers and technology into socio-technical systems that revolutionise the way work is organised and managed. This is an extremely important trend, one that is producing a new model of work relations that will shape the workplace into the 21st century.

This paper examines the challenges being faced by organisations in recent years, reviews some of the responses being taken and presents some case evidence on a job restructuring initiative in one organisation.

THE CHALLENGE TO ORGANISATIONS

Change and Competition

Change has always been a management challenge. However, it may be necessary to make a distinction between what could be described as routine or programmed change and more revolutionary or major non-programmed change. Katzenbach and Smith (1993) define normal change as referring to new circumstances well within the scope of existing management approaches. Such change is dealt with on a daily basis and includes pricing changes, handling disgruntled customers, replacing people and shifting strategic properties. Major change, on the other hand, has become more widespread and it requires individuals throughout the company to become good at behaviours and skills that they may not be very good at. Here one must identify and learn critical new skills and behaviours, and then work to institutionalise those behaviours in order to sustain high performance. The focus must therefore be on values.

As Buchanan and McCalman (1989) highlight, trends in world product markets are encouraging more companies to review their organisational designs, management styles, and employment policies in the interest of more effective asset utilisation, greater flexibility, and product quality and reliability. There is thus a sense in which the organisation cannot look to past practice in order to chart a course for the future, a sense in which the operational parts of the organisation must be re-shaped and adapted in order to aid in the search for competitive advantage. Such re-shaping, it is argued, may need to focus principally on values and value changes.

The Need for Flexibility

In recent years we have witnessed the emergence of a debate among academics, personnel practitioners and the trade union movement on different ways of engaging and utilising labour (Atkinson, 1984; Briggs, 1991; Ackroyd et al, 1988; Gribben, 1992). It would appear that shifts in employment structure and the depressed economic environment have led to a greater variation in the forms of employment, with a trend away from traditional employment arrangements to more "atypical" employment forms, atypical employment being defined as any form of employment which deviates from the full-time permanent format. Accompanying these changes have been significant changes in work patterns. Largely due to the recession of the 1980s, the composition of the workforce has changed. Curson (1986) highlights a number of important trends:

- Commonly experienced reductions in the size of the workforce of companies have led to a reassessment of how to make best use of those employed.

- High unemployment has made unions and employees more concerned and prepared to consider different ways of working in order to retain jobs.

- The creation of a pool of unemployed people means that people are now more prepared to do marginal work such as part-time and temporary work.

- Change in company philosophy often means an increased concentration on the core activities and skills and a willingness to let others provide peripheral services in order to be more flexible and meet demands.

- Increased international competition has led many companies to look at the work patterns of their foreign competitors.

- Market volatility has required more flexibility in response to patterns of demand.

Atkinson (1984) highlights six main drivers of flexibility:

1. *Market Stagnation*: Industry is often too accustomed to rising demand, principally because interruptions to this trend have often been short lived. Also, traditionally, markets have been relatively protected by geographical location. However, the late 1970s brought with them a substantial restriction in market growth in numerous areas. The proliferation of products and services, and tight economic policies have resulted in increased competition for the disposable income available. Hence there are pressures for increased productivity, which traditional working arrangements cannot necessarily deliver. This is exacerbated by global competition, with competitors using cheaper labour to reduce costs.

2. *Employment Costs*: Both redundancy and recruitment are expensive activities, in financial/cost and potentially employee relations

terms. Therefore, varying capacity to match demand by hiring and shedding can have negative results in the longer term. Consequently, organisations are forced to adopt structures which allow them to adjust their capacity with relative ease.

3. *Uncertainty*: Due to market stagnation and heightened competition, organisations require the ability to respond to opportunities and threats as they present themselves. Therefore, in organisation, in technology, in capacity and in skill terms, the firm requires maximum flexibility.

4. *Technological Change*: The ever increasing pace of change in technological developments is forcing radical changes in our approach to work organisation, specifically in relation to the necessity for cross-training and skill flexibility.

5. *Working Time*: Continued reductions in the basic hours worked have forced employers to reconsider the most effective deployment of worked time. Consequently, new and different approaches to structuring work time are appearing.

6. *Industrial Democracy*: The emergence of the so called "new workforce" is bringing with it an increase in the incidence of employee involvement. The call for "industrial citizenship" is accompanied by an expectation of more than just a wage-work bargain relationship. Such a demand cannot be fully met by traditional arrangements.

Overall, therefore, there would appear to be three core imperatives bearing on many businesses: namely, a need to reduce unit costs, a need to respond quickly to environmental changes and a need to meet the demands of the "new" knowledge-based workforce.

The "New" Workforce

One could argue that there has been a general increase in employee expectations over time. This is particularly true in the Irish context with the existence of a large young well educated workforce (Gunnigle and Morley, 1993). Better educated employees can offer employers more. However, they also expect more. Increasingly, many of the most progressive, entrepreneurial and talented people are no longer willing to commit their working lives in a typical pattern to one employer (Brewster et al, 1993). This has had, and continues to have, its influence on management style, contributing to a decline in auto-cratic management. Recent contributions to the debate on change in the workforce, such as those of Vaill (1982), Perry (1984), Kanter (1983) and Quinn-Mills (1991) highlight the need to democratise the workforce in an attempt to make the organisation more effective. This democratisation is necessary in order to develop a highly skilled, flexible, productive workforce and a leaner, more responsive organi-sation. Lawler (1986), commenting on the difference between the "new" organisation and more traditional ones, suggests that:

> almost no aspect of the organisation is left untouched. The nature of jobs, the structure, the reward system, the personnel management system are all changed in significant ways.

He is therefore advocating an integrative approach to the structuring of work and the management of the human factor. Inherent in the con-cept of a "new workforce", according to Mooney (1989), is the notion that a basic reassessment of the value of an individual's worth to the organisation has taken place, with many of the core assumptions of the traditional model being both challenged and rejected. In this re-spect, Mooney suggests that it is important to distinguish between "system" and "value" changes within organisation. A system change simply encompasses changed methodology. Value changes, he sug-gests, on the other hand run deeper. The change from the control (traditional) model to the commitment (new) model is said to be of the second order. Clearly, while system changes are a central focus in the "new" organisation, they are driven by and maintained by a value change in relation to a revised understanding of workplace relations. The traditional notion of an individual as simply an extension of the machine has given way to a belief that employees both feel that work is important and want to contribute to the success of work activity (see Mooney, 1989).

DIMENSIONS OF THE NEW ORGANISATION

The Total Quality Management Environment

The increased emphasis on quality has led many organisations to adopt a total quality management approach in an attempt to provide for full customer satisfaction at sustainable levels of cost. Quality has become a crucial hinge for business success or failure in today's per-formance-oriented markets; a fact that has been emphasised in the literature (Collard, 1989; Develin, 1989; Harrison, 1992). TQM is defined as "zero defects, in the products and services provided by an organisation". Essential to the development of TQM is a recognised quality system. This is an agreed company-wide and plant-wide work structure, documented in effective, integrated, technical and managerial procedures. The quality system co-ordinates the actions of the workforce, the plant and information of the company in the pursuit of customer satisfaction (Feigenbaum, 1983). Therefore, TQM needs to be viewed as a two-part process involving:

- The harnessing of people's commitment to the organisation towards the goal of customer satisfaction.

- The development of systems and procedures which allow for continuous improvement in products or services.

This distinction is vital. New technology, new systems, and new concepts may of themselves produce some improvement in effectiveness, but this result may only be short-run unless sufficient attention is given to harnessing people's commitment.

The Involvement Environment

Employee involvement is a central feature of the new organisational scenario, but clearly conditions must be right for involvement to thrive. In many organisations, involvement has become a buzzword, and although often used, the term is often not understood. Where does meaningful involvement begin? What must organisations be like in order for involvement to occur? Dobbs (1993) suggests that there is often agreement about the way an empowered employee should behave, but much less so on the conditions which are necessary for fostering enough empowerment to change a traditionally hierarchical organisation into a more participative one. He highlights four necessary conditions to encourage empowerment: participation; innovation; access to information; and accountability. These factors combined produce an organisational feeling and "tone" that can have a dramatic, positive effect on employees.

A number of key triggers of involvement can be identified in the literature. Salamon (1992) cites the 1960s and 1970s and the concomitant rise in employee aspirations as the key factor. Others include the issue of industrial alienation (Fox, 1974), the necessity to eliminate poor quality and productivity levels (Lawler, 1986) and the necessity to improve levels of trust between the parties to the labour process (Harrison, 1992).

Conversely, a number of arguments against greater employee involvement have gained prominence over the years. They include the likelihood of a negative impact on unions and union power, principally because forms of involvement such as joint consultation are in effect "duplicate channels of representation". Another criticism is that constant and close relationships between management and employees could lead to a situation where the actions of the two become indivisible. It is suggested that if management and unions have parallel views of success, their relationship may become too "cosy". There is the perception that in such circumstances, it is the union that sacrifices most in terms of risk, but fares worst in the exchange of benefits.

The question of equity in terms of benefits that accrue to management due to involvement initiatives and the rewards offered to unions for their role as facilitators remains a contentious issue. This is especially the case in relation to suggestion schemes and job enrichment initiatives which may save organisations large amounts of money.

Overall, Marchington (1982) maintains that many people give their co-operation to management in terms of involvement at a very "calculative level", principally because there is too much evidence of it being used in a manipulative way and not really contributing to a better work environment or a better power balance in the employment relationship. Consequently, if workplaces continue to stifle enterprise, innovation and intrapreneurship through an unwillingness to engage in "real" involvement initiatives, individuals will continue to go elsewhere to engage in activities that provide them with the stimulus to innovate, where they demonstrate far more skill than most employers encourage them to show at work.

New Organisational Configurations

In recent years there has been a shift in thinking away from the more traditional bureaucratic organisation structures, principally because it is being realised that such hierarchical configurations cannot adequately respond to or anticipate future developments in the business world (Quinn-Mills, 1991; Tiernan, 1993). Quinn-Mills advances the notion of a "cluster structure", a cluster being a group of people drawn from different disciplines, undifferentiated by job title who work together on a semi-permanent basis.

TABLE 1: THE PURE CLUSTER ORGANISATION

♦ Groups undifferentiated by job title working together on a
   semi-permanent basis
♦ Group size varies from 30 to 50 or sub-clusters of 5 to 7
♦ Residual or no hierarchy
♦ No direct reporting relationships
♦ Decision making delegated to lowest possible level, i.e. to
   those who do the work
♦ Leadership rotates to task competence
♦ Members of the group are responsible to the group for
   performance and quality and are therefore accountable
♦ Groups are linked by contacts among members and
   interface with the company through the residual hierarchy.

Source: Quinn-Mills (1991)

Quinn-Mills identifies six advantages that can be achieved by the pure cluster form of organisational structure:

1. The cluster structure results in lower administrative overheads.

2. More entrepreneurial behaviour is witnessed in the cluster organi-sation. Due to the fact that the individual worker is freer to take action and has the necessary skills to do so, innovations and new ideas surface much quicker.

3. Greater flexibility and adaptability are possible with the cluster form of structure.

4. There is more openness to new technology. Reliance is placed on professionals in the cluster structure to keep up to date on advances in technology and the opportunities it can offer.

5. Better retention of workers becomes a reality in the cluster organi-sation. The informality of the cluster organisation helps to attract and retain top employees and to develop assignments that are challenging, varied, and involve working with others.

6. Less promotion risks are found in a cluster structure. With less reliance on advancement up the traditional hierarchy, there is less
   risk of putting people into jobs for which they are not suited.

A cluster develops its own expertise and demonstrates a strong customer orientation. Decision making is pushed to the point of action
and is delegated to the lowest possible level, namely those who complete the work of the organisation. Information is shared freely and the
cluster possesses responsibility and accountability for business results.
Overall, the pure cluster structure allows for the creation of energy or
empowerment, accountability and responsibility which is not possible
in traditional structural forms.

However, the move to pure clusters may be too radical, and some
would argue theory is advancing at a faster pace than practice. In this
respect, Tiernan (1993) suggests that use of the "integrative cluster
structure", a hybrid form of the pure cluster structure in that it builds
on the most important elements of the pure cluster form. Therefore, it
is different to the radical structure advocated by Quinn-Mills. Firstly,
reporting relationships remain in place in this form. Consequently, it
offers a more incremental and gradual approach to organisational restructuring. Secondly, the hierarchy in the integrative cluster structure
is downsized rather than eliminated completely. Tiernan highlights
this as a key criticism of Quinn-Mills proposals. He never makes explicit the degree of hierarchy needed to operate a "pure" cluster
structure. Tiernan's integrative cluster structure points to downsizing
the hierarchy by eliminating layers of middle management and introducing team based work which can either start with the formation of
teams or clusters at the top or bottom. Such teams are overlaid on the
downsized hierarchy but, unlike the pure cluster structure, reporting
relationships still exist.

Work structuring is designed to include the whole task which results in greater flexibility and adaptability and wider career paths resulting in broader experience. Reductions in the administrative hierarchy and formalisation reduce the degree of "bureau psychosis" inherent in more traditional organisational structures. Less hierarchical
control of power is witnessed by pushing decisions down further in
the organisation which enhances autonomy and responsibility for
those involved.

Tiernan also highlights that the teams or clusters also exercise
wider autonomy and responsibility than in the older structural forms.
Such teams should as far as possible be cross-functional and cross-

hierarchical and, in effect, multidisciplinary, which gives rise to enhanced interaction, communication and information flows.

Tiernan concludes that the new organisation is more likely to be
one that has opted for the incremental approach to organisational restructuring, simply because as an approach it is less risky, less radical
and one that may be generally more applicable to industry:

> . . . While providing similar if not the same advantages that the pure
> cluster structure can provide, it avoids the risks and costs of the pure
> cluster structure, and represents a logical progression from traditional bu-
> reaucratic structures to more integrative forms of structure (Tiernan,
> 1993).

Competitive Cultures

The recent literature highlights the importance of a facilitative culture
as a prerequisite to the introduction of other changes (Hofstede, 1991;
Purcell, 1991; Hardscombe and Norman, 1989; Williams, Dobson and
Walters, 1990). As a pattern of shared attitudes, beliefs, assumptions
and expectations, it encompasses the norms and core values of an organisation and manifests itself in the form of organisational climate.

In order for a competitive strategy such as flexibility and for quality to be successful, an appropriate culture is required. An organisation's strategy will dictate a set of critical tasks or objectives that must
be accomplished through a congruence between systems and culture.

Buchanan and McCalman (1989) conducting research at Digital in
Ayr found the concept of organisation culture a slippery one, relatively
difficult to define in theory and difficult to identify in practice. Williams et al (1989) highlight six key characteristics of culture: (1) culture is learnt; (2) culture is both an input and an output; (3) culture is
partly unconscious; (4) culture is historically based; (5) culture is
commonly held rather than shared; and (6) culture is heterogeneous.

Culture assumes significance usually because the strategy of the
organisation, the type of people in power and its structure and systems
reflect the dominant managerial ideology or culture. Furthermore,
such managerial ideologies may be more important than environmental factors in guiding organisational response. Managerial ideology, in recent years, has focused on the core characteristics associated
with the "best run", "achievement oriented", "excellent" organisations. Core dimensions include (1) an action focus, (2) high customer
awareness, (3) intrapreneurship, and (4) autonomy, and therefore by

implication, it is being suggested that a model that assumes low employee commitment simply cannot match the standards of excellence set by world class manufacturers. The overall lesson that emerges from this analysis of best practice, according to Clutterbuck (1985), is that success is characterised by doing "a lot of fairly simple and obvious things well", after all there is relatively little that is revolutionary in the view that individuals give their best when they are treated as caring responsible individuals.

The key concern lies with bringing about cultural change, usually for strategic reasons. Cultural change does not occur in a vacuum, but is often linked to organisational effectiveness via strategic planning. In planning cultural change, organisations need to consider not only how to change the culture of the organisation, but also how to link the change with organisational goals and effectiveness. Cultural change may therefore be driven by business demands. This is clearly significant because business priorities and responses are now changing at a rate much faster than heretofore, with the result that cultural realignment may become the norm rather than the exception. While recognising that the problems of conversion to a new mode of thinking and behaving are significantly smoothed where the pre-existing culture of the organisation is one that is generally receptive to such ideas, value shifts are never easily won (Buchanan and McCalman, 1989).

High Performance Work Structuring

One can distinguish two key approaches to the structuring of work, namely an *individualistic* and a *group* approach, the former examining the possibility of making individual jobs more motivating through an emphasis on individual dispositions and core job characteristics, the latter taking the group as it's primary unit of analysis. In relation to the most recent concept, "high performance work structuring", the central theoretical construct underlying this approach is the achievement of increased commitment and higher productivity through both system and value changes. Therefore, unlike more traditional approaches to job restructuring, which brought with them a system change and/or changed job content, high performance work structuring attempts to bring about a complete value shift (particularly in relation to attitude to organisational systems), along with job content and actual system changes.

This is clearly a new departure, principally because the climate of acceptability for change has altered. The operational problems of

previous years legitimated comparatively limited changes to work structures, while the strategic imperative of the 1990s appears to legitimate more fundamental changes to such structures. As Buchanan and McCalman (1989) highlight:

> It (job restructuring) has tended to be regarded as an isolated management technique aimed at local organisational problems, and at individual jobs, rather than realising that it must be part of a whole company philosophy, through all levels, if it is to be really successful.

Such restructuring is also driven by a revised understanding of workplace relations, on the part of management, with the core features of such new designed plants signalling the direction of the change.

The basic unit of organisation under the high performance mode is the work group. With such primary work groups (between five and 15 people), work is organised around the basic transformations in the process to form whole and complete tasks. Each work group is led by a designated supervisor or facilitator who, along with his team, plans and organises the work within the group itself. Each work group is fully capable of evaluating its performance against standards. Jobs are structured so that work group members can personally control at least one transformation in the process. All work group members have the opportunity to participate formally in the group's common tasks (Garavan and Morley, 1992).

However, developments along such integrated lines that seek to encourage cross-functional flexibility and self-regulating group work must be set within the context of an overall organisational change process involving a redefining of the organisation's philosophy, rather than simply being aimed at individual jobs.

Case Evidence

The foregoing review highlights that the academic literature contends that many changes are taking place. All of these changes point towards the need for organisations to acquire one asset above all else — high calibre people. Clearly individuals will need to possess certain characteristics, regardless of the level at which they operate in the organisational hierarchy. Not least among those characteristics are the following:

- A high level of education. This education will have to cover both technical skills and broader business issues because employees will

be required to operate new technology, understand their role in the wider organisation context and be capable of taking decisions on their own.

- An ability to learn new skills and continually adapt to changing circumstances. This will clearly require the individual to take responsibility for their own development, learn new processes and keep skills up to date.

- An ability to work without supervision including the self monitoring of performance. Such self management will allow organisations to create the flexibility needed to remove layers of management and introduce the types of changes outlined earlier.

- Well developed interpersonal skills in order to facilitate the management of the internal and external customer interface.

- An ability to solve problems and think creatively about future possibilities and contribute to change in the organisation (see Morley and Garavan, 1993).

The case study to be presented in the remainder of this paper is set in the context of a high-technology work environment. It explores some of the issues involved in organisational change and development at different levels, with particular reference to the introduction of teams at the production level. It examines both the system and the value changes that accompany a job restructuring intervention, and allows the reader to observe, in a concrete manner, some of the outcomes of this type of change.

Company X, a unionised organisation with headquarters in the United States, is a manufacturer of computer systems and associated equipment. Founded in the 1970s, the company has been actively involved in building computer networks for more than fifteen years. The company operates in highly competitive circumstances, and its external environment is both complex and dynamic. The company appreciates that organisational change is necessary in order to remain a market leader.

During 1991 the company changed its pricing strategy, distribution strategy and overall financial model, as well as commencing to change job structures and the way work is completed, all in an effort to win new customers and ensure greater success in the marketplace.

One selected area in the manufacturing facility was re-organised into teams of 6-15 members. For research purposes a series of naturally occurring groups were identified (N=50). Since the research occurred in a natural setting, participants could not be randomly allocated to the groups. The groups were simply identified in the organisation in terms of whether they were going to be exposed to the restructuring programme. Clearly therefore, some degree of control over extraneous variables, relative to that possible in a true experiment, is lost due to the lack of complete equivalence.

Four sets of measures relating to the following areas were taken during the study:

- Culture and value changes (using Shaskins 1984 Organisational Beliefs Instrument).

- Work characteristics and satisfaction changes (using scales developed by Hackman and Lawler, 1971 and 1976).

- Commitment changes (using desire and intent to remain with the organisation as outcome measures of commitment).

- High performance organisation characteristics (using scales developed by Buchanan and McCalman, 1989).

CULTURE AND VALUE CHANGE

Overall with respect to culture and value changes (Table 2), the results reveal that of the ten dimensions measured by the Organisational Beliefs Instrument, there was an improvement in six. Those dimensions involved a belief in:

- the importance of having fun through ones work

- the importance of people as individuals

- superior quality and service

- the importance of economic growth and profits

- the importance of hands on management

- the importance of a recognised organisational philosophy.

TABLE 2:
CULTURE AND VALUE CHANGES

(N=50)	Time 1 Mean	SD	Time 2 Mean	SD	T Value
A belief in the importance of having fun through one's work	3.852	0.467	4.076	0.539	2.030**
A belief in being the best at what the company does	3.832	0.253	3.516	0.146	-7.38**
A belief that people in the organisation should be innovators and take risks without feeling that they will be punished if they fail	3.546	0.306	3.640	0.140	0.770 NS
A belief in the importance of attending to details in doing a job	3.252	0.416	3.336	0.278	1.240 NS
A belief in the importance of people as individuals	3.184	0.277	3.388	0.110	5.410***
A belief in superior quality and service	3.232	0.298	3.406	0.246	4.160***
A belief in the importance of informality to improve the flow of communication through the organisation	3.269	0.220	3.556	0.222	1.750 NS
A belief in the importance of economic growth and profits	3.440	0.124	3.820	0.243	7.790***
A belief in the importance of hands-on management, the notion that managers should be doers, not just planners and administrators	3.148	0.303	3.472	0.180	6.680***
A belief in the importance of a recognised organisational philosophy developed and supported by those at the top	3.272	0.419	3.460	0.236	3.370**

*** $P < 0.001$; ** $P < 0.001$; * $P < 0.05$; NS Not Significant

Three dimensions remained unchanged. They were:

- a belief that people in the organisation should be innovators and should take risks without feeling that they will be punished if they fail

- a belief in the importance of attending to details in doing a job

- a belief in the importance of informality to improve the flow of communication through the organisation. Finally, the results suggest that one belief has disimproved i.e. a belief in being the best at what the company does.

Overall the results point up job restructuring as an overarching concept which contains not only system, methodology and job content concerns, but also implications for the organisation's value and belief system, a concept not widely examined in the extant literature. Few researchers have examined the idea of a value shift accompanying changes in job restructuring, and the importance of a good fit between an organisation's approach to work structuring and its belief system.

WORK CHARACTERISTICS AND SATISFACTION CHANGES

TABLE 3:
WORK CHARACTERISTICS AND SATISFACTION

(N=50)	Time 1		Time 2		
	Mean	*SD*	*Mean*	*SD*	*T Value*
Work Variety	1.880	1.069	3.860	0.351	12.370***
Satisfaction with work allocation	2.240	0.573	3.400	0.833	7.900***
Suggestion/idea input	1.760	0.687	3.800	0.728	14.01***
Satisfaction with working conditions	3.840	0.818	4.820	0.671	5.320**
Satisfaction with feedback on performance	1.940	0.424	4.300	0.863	16.27***
Satisfaction with job security	2.120	0.799	3.540	0.813	8.770***
Autonomy	1.720	0.743	3.250	0.354	16.04***

*** P < 0.001; ** P < 0.01; * P < 0.05; NS Not Significant

Overall the results regarding changes to work satisfaction are very positive, most probably because they are supported by and congruent with the emerging beliefs now espoused by the organisation. Following the introduction of teams, both work variety and autonomy have improved significantly. This participative approach is serving to create a better work environment in which individuals feel that they have at least some input. This is illustrated by a comment made by an operator:

> "It (the work group intervention) has given us control of how we do our own jobs. It is no longer a matter of just doing what the supervisor says." (Operator)

When questioned about who is really responsible for the quality of product, the following comments are typical of the replies given:

> "Everyone plays a part in the quality of the department, from management to operators on the floor." (Supervisor)

> "We are all responsible in our own area of work. We make our own job aids, so therefore we know what faults to look for. If each person does their job, then we would have no need to still have QA. But at the moment we still have a QA station for spot checks. But I myself think that it is down to us all to set our own quality standards." (Operator)

Clearly, it would appear that individuals are aware of their responsibility in this area and have the ability to express this.

Similarly, individuals were asked "Do you check your own work? Should you, or should someone else?" The responses were similar, including comments such as:

> "Yes, I check my own work and so should everyone else. Otherwise there would be no interest or responsibility in what is being done." (Operator)

> "I think we are each responsible for our own work. If you set high standards for yourself, then you expect it from the next person, and so on down the line, and if you have a problem with someone's work being careless, then I would have no problem in saying it to that operator." (Operator)

In relation to satisfaction with feedback on performance, the results reveal a marked improvement. This may potentially be explained by the redeployment of a second supervisor to the area, which resulted in both individual supervisors having more time to dedicate to giving the

teams feedback on their performance. Prior to the restructuring intervention, this had been highlighted as a particular problem area, with
94 per cent of those individuals surveyed being either dissatisfied or
very dissatisfied with the amount of feedback on performance they
received from their supervisor.

The results also reveal a marked improvement in satisfaction with
work allocation. One possible explanation for this result may be the
fact that individuals are now being constantly updated on what has
been achieved in the past and what had to be achieved in the future,
coupled with a rationale for such targets. Prior to this, individuals
would have been much less aware of the reasons for completing certain tasks, of fluctuations in demand, of the sales achieved for particular periods and so forth. Furthermore, in relation to satisfaction with
work allocation, because individuals are now working in teams, the
burden of responsibility is shared, and a shared sense of purpose
seems to have emerged.

> "They (work teams) help in achieving the end product easier. They help a
> lot of people to mix with people they would otherwise not be in contact
> with." (Operator)

> "The work teams involve everyone in making the department work out
> right. Everyone feels wanted." (Operator)

> "The work teams are a great idea. I myself am involved in a team. We
> discuss what needs to be done and who does what. Some people might
> have a problem, so we all try to give an idea on how best to tackle the
> problem." (Operator)

Suggestion/idea input has also improved considerably. The pre-results
revealed that 90 per cent of those surveyed were either dissatisfied, or
very dissatisfied with the way their suggestions and ideas were used.
The post results suggest that only 16 per cent remain dissatisfied.

There has always been a suggestion scheme in operation at the
plant and its operation has not changed. However, individuals at lower
levels in the organisation are now much more involved in process improvement and idea generation than heretofore. Weekly meetings are
held in which individuals are encouraged to make suggestions which
are then evaluated by fellow team members. This clearly has resulted
in individuals being given much greater opportunities for involvement. It has also resulted in a "healthy" degree of competition be-

tween groups, particularly in relation to arriving at solutions to "house keeping" problems.

Overall, the results from the present study lend support to the proposition of a net advantage in moving towards a high performance work system, with respect to individuals experiencing greater work variety and autonomy on their jobs, greater involvement and sugges-tion/idea input and greater satisfaction with how work is allocated and with the amount of feedback on performance received. Concomitantly, the literature suggests that it is characteristics such as these which draw out and "satisfy the individuals higher needs" (Cooper, 1977).

COMMITMENT CHANGES

Desire and intent to remain with the organisation were investigated to test for outcomes of commitment. The author was trying to establish whether there was a change in either the respondents desire or intent to remain with the organisation as a result of the job restructuring in-tervention. The results reveal that while there was an improvement in the group's desire to remain with the organisation, there was no change in the group's intent to remain.

TABLE 4:
COMMITMENT

	Time 1		Time 2		
(N=50)	Mean	SD	Mean	SD	T Value
Desire to remain with the organisation	2.858	0.162	3.109	0.148	7.420***
Intent to remain with the organisation	2.810	0.381	2.950	0.403	1.850 NS

*** P < 0.001; ** P < 0.01; * P < 0.05; NS Not Significant

At Company X the increase in the individual's desire to remain with the organisation may partially have come about as a result of the enskilling programme and as a result of the better person-environment fit being created. Furthermore, the job restructuring initiative is one without a hidden agenda. Individuals are clearly aware of why the or-ganisation is taking this route. It has explicitly been told that work teams are "an attempt to harness peoples commitment to drive pro-ductivity and quality, and to encourage people's participation in decision making and promote job enrichment". It clearly has not been sold as something that will benefit them only, and those responsible for driving the initiative have not neglected to mention the potential productivity and quality benefits that could accrue.

It is interesting to note that intent to remain with the organisation has not significantly changed. In this authors opinion, a potential explanation for this may well lie in rational choice theory (Rose, 1975; Willener, 1970). It was noted that desire to remain had improved, potentially as a result of the new order being constructed in the organisation, but in relation to intent to remain, rational choice seems to suggest that individuals actions are generally presumed to be rational, and the individual will generally act in accordance with his own interpretations of the situation. Therefore asking the individual about their intent to remain with the organisation poses some difficulty as the individual will only remain if it is advantageous to do so. The individual may well have a desire to remain for various reasons, but if it is advantageous to go, then he/she may well do so.

HIGH PERFORMANCE ORGANISATION CHARACTERISTICS

The latter part of this study sought to identify the impact of the changes on the high performance approach to work (see Table 5). Using the scales identified by Buchanan and McCalman (1989), the items fell into seven main categories, concerning teamwork, relationships, high performance, autonomy, management style, work itself, and opportunities for growth and advancement. The pre-responses indicated that the individual's expectations of how successful the work teams would be were very high, with individuals on the whole suggesting that they felt that the work teams would work and morale in them would be high, relationships would improve, there would be high standards of performance, greater autonomy, a participative management style, more interesting and varied work, better supervision and feedback, and better opportunities for growth and advancement. The post results reveal that the teams expectations were realised, with the improvement occurring in all items proving highly significant.

In relation to teamwork, the pattern of responses suggest that the teams are working well and that individuals expectations are being satisfied in this regard. Problem solving, flexibility and co-ordination are issues which continue to be handled well in the high performance environment.

Turning to relationships, the results indicate that shared responsibility, information sharing and mutual trust and confidence are now characteristic of relationships in the department.

With respect to high performance, the two key items used in the questionnaire ("There is greater opportunity for people to grow as a result of the introduction of teams", and "People in my team do maintain high standards of performance"), are according to Buchanan and McCalman (1989), key items which concern core "values" of high performance work systems. Accordingly, they suggest that if the high performance approach was not working effectively, then this would have been revealed most directly in responses to these items. In the present study the pattern of responses suggests that the values are strong after the introduction of work teams.

TABLE 5:
HIGH PERFORMANCE ORGANISATION CHARACTERISTICS

(N=50)	Time 1		Time 2		
	Mean	SD	Mean	SD	T Value
Teamwork	3.310	0.541	4.005	0.439	7.410***
Relationships	3.115	0.676	3.870	0.282	7.220***
High Performance	2.850	0.455	4.460	0.244	21.19***
Autonomy	3.433	0.754	3.933	0.294	4.110***
Management Style	3.265	0.598	3.840	0.479	5.720***
Work itself	30.40	0.826	4.380	0.594	9.130***
Opportunities for Growth	2.960	0.989	4.500	0.505	9.220***
Opportunities for Advancement	2.340	1.154	2.980	0.551	3.740***

*** P < 0.001; ** P < 0.01; * P < 0.05; NS Not Significant

Turning to autonomy, the new work teams structure appears to have enhanced the personal responsibility of the teams and has given them greater freedom to work without too much supervision. Again this is a dynamic which is seen as central to the development of a high performance approach to work.

Under the heading "Management Style", the pattern of responses to these items reinforces the participative management perception of team work, and the necessity for appropriate consultation and feedback and equality in disciplinary matters. However, on one of these items (I am treated fairly when I do something wrong), 64 per cent of respondents answered "not sure" in the time 2 questionnaire. This may be indicative of some dissatisfaction with management practice in this area. On the whole however, there were few negative responses to these items.

The work itself appears to have increased in both variety and interest, confirming results presented in section two on "Work Characteristics and Satisfaction". Qualitative data on the same items revealed the following:

"I like it because I have a deal of variety." (Operator)

"The best is the variety of things I can do on my own initiative." (Operator)

Opportunity for growth, again according to Buchanan and McCalman, is another core value of high performance work systems, and the pattern of responses to this item suggests that the value is held by employees, with 100 per cent of respondents either agreeing or strongly agreeing with the statement that "the new team structure has made better use of my abilities".

In relation to opportunities for advancement, there was an improvement, but not to the same extent as occurred in opportunities for growth. Only 12 per cent agreed with the statement that "the new team structure has improved my promotion opportunities", while 88 per cent were either "not sure", or "disagreed". However, in this respect, it is also important to note that neither was this expectation high prior to the intervention. Only 20 per cent of respondents agreed with the statement that "the new team structure will improve my promotion opportunities", while 28 per cent were not sure, and 52 per cent either disagreed or strongly disagreed.

In summary, the results reveal that the job restructuring initiative has attracted the positive commitment and enthusiasm of those exposed to it. However a word of warning needs to be sounded. Lawler (1986) predicts that the approach can decay, and that management can regress as production problems and other priorities and preoccupations divert time and other resources to other activities and projects.

The high performance concept will rarely survive under traditional management and as Buchanan and McCalman (1989) point out "can thus be expected to revert to the prevailing norms in the absence of special attention to maintain it's special features".

Clearly, however, it remains to be seen whether this new way of working continues to form part of everyday operations, or whether there will be a revert back to more traditional patterns of working. Positive factors weighing in on the side of the teams remaining successful include firstly, the witnessing of a value shift among those concerned, and secondly, the fact that the work teams have been introduced into the organisation as a pro-active measure, and not simply as a response to a particular problem.

THE TRANSITION TO THE NEW ORGANISATION

The guiding principles for the emergence of the "new" organisation are indeed compelling ones. The challenge of un-programmed change, the necessity for flexibility and the ability to respond positively to the changing priorities of the "new workforce" are all issues that require strong coping mechanisms. It is in this coping that organisations succeed or fail. The problem for most organisations lies in what is described as "transition management" (Perry, 1984; Buchanan and McCalman, 1989). It is comparatively straightforward to identify the work and organisational design features that one wishes to implement. There is general agreement among both academics and practitioners of the value to be gained from moving towards a total quality environment, of the necessity for "real" employee involvement, at least in some areas, of the advantages to be gained by structural de-layering, of the benefits of a strong culture and of the practical consequences of high performance oriented work structuring. However, the main problem lies in determining how to take an organisation and its members through the transition. This is a high risk venture, one that involves the creation and communication of a number of different vision sets dedicated to the changing of all aspects of the organisational system (how quality is viewed; how much responsibility is to be accorded to individuals; and how the structure, culture and work system reflect this). This is a venture that involves the changing of what has been "a way of life".

6

The Management of Change:
The Pfizer Case Study

Joe Cogan
Managing Director,
Pfizer Pharmaceuticals

PERSONAL EXPERIENCE OF CHANGE

Over a period of 34 years in industry — living in Ireland, UK, main-land Europe and the USA — I have worked for four companies, in two of them for 28 years. If I count the divisions and subsidiaries of those two companies, Unilever and Pfizer, in which I spent those 28 years and with which I had assignments or substantial involvements, the number comes to 18. Of those 18, only 8 remain in any recognisable form and those 8 have changed radically.

Some of those businesses were overwhelmed by changes in the business environment so great that they could not adapt — and they sank. Some shrunk from being manufacturers to distributors. Some merged with other companies. Some expanded from little local businesses to world-wide international market leaders. Those that have survived have changed so utterly that they would virtually be unrecognisable today by comparison to 20 years ago. In some cases, competitive pressures, problems of profitability and imminent threat of extinction were the motives for change. In the most successful and the strongest, the impetus came from the early recognition of the need for change and the embedding of continuous change in the organisation's culture.

The only really important job of management, after making enough money to pay employees, suppliers, the government and shareholders, is to initiate and implement change. I find it quite difficult, therefore, to separate the management of change from the general process of management. Management is, as business is, mostly about change.

In the industrial relations context, if I am allowed a few observations and pleas they would be these: because continuous systematic change is essential for the survival and prosperity of business and for employment, it is in everyone's interest that it should be encouraged. Employees have the right to be critical of managements that do not initiate change. Pay bargaining practices that inhibit change should be abandoned. Productivity bargaining practices that store up changes for later negotiation in return for increases in pay and benefits should be discouraged by both unions and employees. I would also make a plea to eliminate those forms of union organisation that restrict what a person can do by defending boundaries of demarcation. Not only do these inhibit the development of competitive organisations by resisting change institutionally, but they limit the scope, growth and rewards of the very people they are supposed to protect.

REASONS FOR CHANGE

In business, the motivation for change usually comes from competitive pressures, either immediate or long term. Responses are manifested in the desire to gain advantage or just keep up with technological developments in product design or manufacturing techniques; to improve quality and customer service; to reduce costs; and, the key to most of the others, to improve the culture of the organisation. The various factors — technology, organisation, competitive exposure, culture — all interact. Big changes can occur, for example, in the culture of an organisation by its becoming exposed to greater competition or by radically changing the technology, without ever consciously setting out to change the culture. Likewise, a deliberate and successful attempt to change culture can *improve* the innovative performance of an organisation and make it more responsive to the external environment and more competitive. But bringing about such change in the absence of an immediate threat to the survival of the organisation is, in my experience, usually quite difficult.

STRATEGIES FOR CHANGE

As there are many reasons for changes and many different circumstances in which those needs arise, there are many strategic options. The strategy can vary from a long-term, incremental, participative ("let's do it together") type to quick and coercive ("we do this now or else we're all dead") type. Each has its own place and will depend on such considerations as the nature of the change required, urgency, the number of people needed to make the change, the means and information possessed by those wanting to make the change, the resistance expected, etc. Some strategies would, of course, be incompatible with certain goals, as would a coercive approach in the context of a participative organisation culture.

A DESIGN FOR CHANGE

In my experience, all successfully managed change has a number of stages and features in common, as follows:

Stages
- recognition of the need
- elaboration of the need (diagnosis — what's wrong)
- gaining "political" support
- developing plans
- implementing plans and monitoring progress
- reassessment and adjustment

Qualities
- leadership and persistence
- authenticity and credibility
- thorough communications
- flexibility in implementation

An Example from Pfizer, Ringaskiddy

In the late 1970s Pfizer, Ringaskiddy employed almost 780 people in the manufacture of fine chemicals and bulk pharmaceuticals. The plant was overstaffed; absenteeism was over 11 per cent; there were regular disputes and stoppages; a myriad of work restrictions and malpractices existed; there were frequent disciplinary incidents. Much management time was wasted in dealing with industrial relations issues. Productivity was low by comparison with other Pfizer plants and reliability of shipments was unsatisfactory. Either we change this state of affairs or there would be no money for reinvestment and, sooner or later, we would crumble out of business.

The system then was not conducive to change through participation. Many of the shop stewards had been for too long fighting for the retention of old work practices and restrictions to adapt. Other shop stewards, and most employees who were naturally apprehensive in a struggle for power where the credibility of management after years of appeasement was in doubt and the outcome was uncertain, naturally preferred to hedge their bets. The situation called for a "firm" approach.

A plan was prepared identifying more efficient manning arrangements, unacceptable work restrictions and malpractices, procedures and codes for handling absenteeism and disciplinary situations. Training was given to supervisory personnel. A voluntary severance plan was introduced. A new pay and benefits agreement, bringing sensible improvements, was negotiated.

Changes in working arrangements and practices were introduced on a phased basis. There was resistance, of course. Some resulted in short work stoppages. The changes identified were nevertheless introduced.

In three years, absenteeism declined from more than 11 per cent to less than 5 per cent. Total manpower was down to 606 and production was up more than 26 per cent — an increase in output per person of 65 per cent. Pay and benefits were improved. In the voluntary redundancy programme many people who were not well matched to the necessary disciplines of industrial life, left to do their things. We lost many very suitable people too, people who had too much of the strife and tension caused by the previous climate. Most of the remaining employees believed the changes to be essential. Mutual respect between employees and management improved.

More than 10 years have passed since then. Many tens of millions of pounds have been invested. Pfizer has since sold its food chemical business to ADM. The pharmaceutical plant, now Pfizer Pharmaceuticals, employs 240 people, more than it even did before, and is growing. Productivity has grown many fold. Absenteeism is 2 per cent. Our safety record is well below the industry average. A "disciplinary incident" is almost unheard of. Most employees are shareholders in the company. Our reputation as a reliable, quality supplier within Pfizer is very good. We are currently investing more than £100 million. We have a number of successful and unique new products that will be the basis for our future security and expansion.

In this climate of advantage we are engaged in efforts to improve our organisation culture — the way we do things here — to one that is more participative and involved, where there is trust and mutual respect, where change is assimilated without anxiety and resistance, where a dispute would be seen as a failure by all concerned, where people get more than their wage packet from their work and achieve a sense of pride and recognition.

These ideals cannot be realised by coercion; they must be desired by the majority. Thus, this effort is being directed by a steering committee drawn from people across the organisation. In the 18 months since the establishment of this committee, 90 recommendations have been issued covering everything from communications, management visibility, the running of social and family events to operational matters; 82 have been implemented. A training programme dealing with effectiveness in group activity and collaboration, involving every employee, was recommended by the employees' steering committee and is well underway. Employees now engage in the selection of new employees, they conduct safety audits, they participate in constructive criticism of the way we do things and make helpful suggestions. All this will not turn a job in a factory, with all the necessary regimes and disciplines and some drudgery at least, into Utopia. Will it really change things? I believe it will.

PART TWO

WORLD CLASS MANUFACTURING AND THE IMPLICATIONS FOR INDUSTRIAL RELATIONS

7

World Class Manufacturing and the Implications for Industrial Relations

John Geary

Department of Industrial Relations,
University College Dublin

INTRODUCTION

In recent years, there has been a significant increase in employers' interest in the re-organisation of work. New labels abound: just-in-time, cellular manufacturing, lean production, human resource management, total quality management, team working and, more recently, world class manufacturing. Although the meaning ascribed to these various practices varies notably from one European country to another, they all speak of the need for a new management strategy which no longer relies on merely securing employees' compliance but seeks instead to win over their consent and commitment. It has become common for management to claim that the old adversarial style of industrial relations has been replaced by a strategy which seeks to win over the hearts and minds of employees by developing an individualised relationship between them and their employers.

DEFINING OUR TERMS

With this multitude of labels and associated definitions I have found it more useful to speak of "new forms of work organisation". This has two elements: the technical organisation of work which refers to an organisation's plant, equipment and production methodologies; and the social organisation of work which relates to the manner in which people are grouped around a given technology.

More precisely, I define the latter as opportunities which management provide at workplace level for consultation with and/or delegation of responsibilities and authority for decision-making to their sub-

ordinates either as individuals or as groups of employees relating to
the immediate work situation and are invited to participate in decisions which relate to the organisation of work at the point of production. Thus, workers may influence the manner in which work is allocated, the scheduling of work and when to take breaks. They are also
actively encouraged to seek solutions to problems and to make suggestions which will improve the organisation's efficiency. This, of
course, means that workers are expected to adopt the ends of the enterprise as their own: workers' interests and those of their employer
are to be inextricably linked. New forms of work organisation are
used thus as a means of generating employee commitment, motivation
and co-operation. It is an effort on management's part to gain employees' active consent and to persuade them to work hard and diligently.

This paper reviews the implementation of new forms of work organisation in Britain, but it also makes reference to experience elsewhere in Europe. It begins by briefly considering how employers' interest in work organisation has changed in recent years. The second
section looks at new forms of work organisation in practice by examining its impact on the shop-floor and the manner in which it effects
employees' and managers' working lives. In the third section, I extend
my brief somewhat and examine the implications of new forms of
work organisation for industrial relations practices and procedures.
The final section looks at a number of key questions which employers
and trade unions are likely to face in the coming years.

CHANGING CONTEXTS: CHANGING APPROACHES

The lack of stable markets and the erosion of firms' competitive position, together with the introduction of new technologies, has compelled employers to look again at the technical and social organisation
of work in their enterprises. These new competitive pressures have
forced companies to reduce costs, raise productivity, improve quality,
delayer management and achieve greater flexibility in the deployment
of labour. The need to maximise the potential of each individual employee is paramount. The telling lesson comes from Japan, where an
important reason for Japanese competitive advantage, it is claimed,
lies in the organisation of production, a vital constituent of which is
the greater involvement of employees in their work; often organised
into production teams which overcome many of the inefficiencies associated with traditional forms of work organisation.

In its more sophisticated form, the evidence in Britain would suggest that new forms of work organisation are largely confined to a small number of well-publicised companies, many of which were originally established on greenfield sites, like Rothmans, Trebor, Whitbread and Fisher Body. Japanese companies like Nissan, Komatsu, Hitachi and Matsushita also figure prominently here. Indeed, these incoming Japanese companies have often inspired indigenous firms to experiment with new production methodologies and new forms of work organisation. On brown field sites, however, change has of necessity been more gradual. Recent examples of trade union agreements to introduce new working practices and methods of production include Ford, IBC, BP Chemicals, Rover, Vauxhall, Rolls Royce, Cadbury Schweppes, Wandsworth Health Authority, JCB, Pirelli, Hoover, BICC, Cummins Engines, Jaguar, Lucas Automotive and Lucas Aerospace. Of course, it is another matter whether these agreements have, or will culminate in significant change on the shop floor.

IMPACT ON EMPLOYEES

There is substantial agreement that, while changes to production technologies have offered employees some benefits in the form of new skills and responsibilities, they have also been accompanied by certain undesirable effects. The main effects that new work structures have had on employees are listed below:

1. *The Formalisation of Procedures*: The first and perhaps most profound impact new work structures have had on employees' work relates to the manner in which employers seek to extract effort from their employees. Increasingly, management rely less on informal rules and understandings and more on strictly defined procedures and norms.

2. *Change for Everyone?* The second point to note is that the development of new working arrangements has not improved the lot of semi-skilled and un-skilled workers a great deal. Skilled workers have been far more likely to experience skill enhancement and increased responsibility. And as women continue to occupy the majority of un-skilled and semi-skilled jobs, the gender divide, too, would seem to have been left relatively untouched. Thus, established forms of work organisation and hierarchical relations con-

tinue to be reproduced. Despite this, however, it cannot be presumed that skilled employees have not lost out in some respects as a result of work organisation changes. Intermediate specialist groups, like engineers, accountants and skilled manual employees, who formerly enjoyed considerable autonomy, have had many of their privileges withdrawn. In an attempt to bring these groups under tighter managerial control, they have been transferred to line positions and exposed to the regulation of production. No longer are they permitted to reside within specialist functions or departments: the locus of their identities shifts from a profession or an occupation towards the needs of production. Thus, the paradox of "team working", for these employees at least, is that it not only restricts their autonomy, but it also fragments their collective identity and isolates them from their colleagues. The problem for management with their former "team orientation" is that it exists apart from managerial priorities and the "new" team working strategy is, therefore, directed towards reconstituting one team identity for another.

3. *Less Autonomy*: The evidence suggests that the introduction of new production technologies has had ambiguous effects on employees' autonomy. For instance, with modular manufacturing where there are two or more cells (i.e. where each cell is responsible for a discrete part of the products' manufacture), the level of overall coordination and task interdependence increases and employees' discretion over the pace and methods of work is restrained. The introduction of JIT, too, has been found to reduce employees' autonomy. Unlike traditional methods of production which permit the insertion of buffer inventories between successive stages of the production process and allow for variability in the time and pace of production, JIT seeks to reduce slack and variability by establishing a high degree of standardisation throughout the production process. But as inventory levels are reduced, and as the right amount of product has to be produced at just the right time, so the pace and time of production remains outside of employees' control.

There is also a considerable amount of evidence which would suggest that management continue to use other, more traditional forms of control. Close policing of time-keeping, attendance and breaks has become commonplace. Nissan, a company which it is claimed has transformed the social relations of production by introducing team working, *inter alia,* continues to maintain close forms of supervision — a ratio of 20:1. This would suggest that conventional forms of authority relations persist even where one might most have expected new forms of work organisation to have ordained the reverse. Thus, while some employers emphasise team working and employee participation, alongside them exists a regime that is overtly based on an assertion of managerial control.

4. *Effort Intensification*: New production methodologies have also been associated with increased anxiety and stress in the workplace. With JIT, for example, as employees are expected to dispense with traditional notions of what constitutes "hard work" , they are required to engage in other activities which might lead to improvements in the production process. The pressures associated with these changes represent an intensification of effort levels, not as commonly understood by the term, but perceived by employees to be sufficient to detract from, or outweigh, the other benefits associated with new forms of work organisation. These new pressures have not been confined to shop-floor employees alone. Managers and indirect staff, too, have suffered from stress in introducing and in trying to adapt to and maintain these new forms of work organisation. Of course, job intensification can and does arise from other aspects of job restructuring, apart from JIT. Some commentators have argued that management's primary objective in enlarging jobs and in increasing labour's flexibility has not been to enhance peoples' skills but rather to increase work loads and reduce the amount of spare or free time available to employees. While some employers will certainly go down this route, other employers will wish to improve productivity through the introduction of new production methodologies and new work structures, and it is by no means inevitable that employees will necessarily perceive this to be undesirable or unacceptable. There are two reasons for this. First, as the introduction of new work practices is often accompanied by the removal of piece rates, and as the production flow becomes more balanced, the pressure on un-skilled and semi-skilled employees in particular will have been reduced. Second, where the organisation of production leads to a more systematic and better planned manufacturing process and to a reduction in overtime working, it is

conceivable that employees would also look upon this as a decrease in effort levels.

5. *A Transformation in Employees' Attitudes?* There is considerable agreement that, in spite of managements' efforts to change the structure of work, employees' trust has not increased significantly: the "them and us" syndrome remains stubbornly persistent. There are a number of reasons for this.

a) Lack of Choice: Employees have often had little say in the decision to adopt new forms of work organisation and have rarely had a choice whether they can participate or not once they are implemented.

b) Lack of Trust: This lack of trust has two dimensions: (i) can management be believed that it is *motivated* to do what it says and (ii) can it be trusted that it is *able* to do what it says.

c) Unequal Outcomes: Who is to benefit in terms of employment, pay etc. Union demands for a future stake in Aer Lingus is an example here: "for having taken the pain, let's share the gain".

d) Lack of Institutional Support: This relates to a lack of senior management commitment to the change programme.

e) Lack of Integration with Personnel Management Policy: An example here is at one of Lucas' plants in Birmingham, where it was found that, while employees welcomed team working, the lack of resources allocated to training prevented them from acquiring a wider repertoire of skills to rotate between work tasks within the manufacturing cell. Also, the flattening of job hierarchies, which is often associated with new forms of work organisation has been found to induce discontent amongst employees by removing promotion opportunities. Thus, there is an inherent tension between the need to reduce the number of job descriptions in order to promote flexibility, and the need to retain these job hierarchies so as to enlist employees' ideological and normative commitment.

f) An Introverted Loyalty: One unanticipated consequence of new forms of work organisation is that employees' commitment and loyalty is sometimes directed inwards towards the immediate work team and co-operation between work groups is prevented as a result. Thus, employees' favourable response to new forms of work organisation is not generalised to affect their wider relationship with management.

In summary, it is clear that the changing nature of competition has forced employers to look closely at their work organisation strategies. To suggest, however, that these pressures have led to a transformation in the way in which labour is managed would be to err. Management are certainly determined to eradicate any obstacles that may prohibit them from improving the manner in which people work. But they are *against* restrictive practices and inflexibilities, rather than positively *for* creating new skill structures. Despite all the talk and enthusiasm for change, then, employers' interest in implementing change has been confined to the margins of existing working practices and attempts to embrace new forms of work organisation have been remarkably rare. Thus, change has not affected employees' lives a great deal. There has been little significant upskilling and, for the main part, task specialisation and gendered divisions of labour have remained as they were. Traditional modes of control have remained important, too. Close forms of supervision, job intensification, and strict policing of attendance and of hours coming to and from work would all suggest that the manner in which the shop floor order is constructed bears a close resemblance with past practice. Management's attitude to new working practices would appear to be ambivalent, perhaps governed basically by the question of which course — specialisation of skills with inflexibility or multiskilling with additional training — will cost more.

REACTION OF MANAGERS

It has been widely recognised that management commitment and support is the *sine qua non* for the success of new forms of work organisation. The failure of past initiatives, likely quality circles has been explained by a managerial failure to understand the necessity of a *total* system of quality and business improvement and for not having given adequate attention to adapting organisational structures and personnel policies. Circles were adopted as island solutions. They were also seen to disrupt managers' lives for sparse returns and created an organisational complexity that confused existing structures. Senior management, too, were seen to lack the necessary resolve and commitment to make them work. Thus, in a situation where senior management fail to make the necessary organisational changes and are equivocal in their support, one might expect middle management to think it rational not to support the changes.

But even in instances where senior management have been committed to introducing new forms of work organisation, middle and line management indifference and resistance has shown itself to be a significant impediment. Line management's fear that the extension and involvement of employees in decision-making procedures would threaten their traditional right to manage has been a prominent factor in explaining the failure of these initiatives. Moreover, employees' suggestions for improving the manner in which work is organised may not only be seen as a criticism of managers' performance, but if employees continue to identify problems and implement solutions, supervisors, in particular, may *fear* for their future employment.

In other situations, too, an extension in employees' participation may be prevented by management's fear that, although these new participative structures permit them increased involvement in decision-making procedures both with their superiors and with other managers from other departments, it allows their counterparts from other areas to interfere into what has been hitherto the preserve of their discretion.

Important though these considerations are, it would seem that management have often been more concerned to conform to fashion when adopting new forms of work organisation initiatives and have not been acting from conviction. There is also the urgency with management in general, and within personnel management in particular, to be seen to be doing something effective and relevant: that change is less dramatic than may have been expected is often less important than the symbolic meaning attached to managerial action. At a more fundamental level, the evidence would also suggest that British management, in contrast to other European countries, has rarely fashioned a debate which portrays the possibility of delegative participation on the one hand, and centralised management control on the other, as representing credible alternatives. It is more the case that management chose the latter as a matter of course rather than as a preference following deliberate and considered debate of the merits of other possible approaches.

IMPLICATIONS FOR INDUSTRIAL RELATIONS

Although there has been little research on this subject, we do know that, despite the increase in managerial power throughout the 1980s, employers have rarely sought to, or wished to, remove trade unions completely from their enterprises. When introducing change it has been more typical of employers to try to bring their work force and its representatives along with them. "Involvement" and "participation" have become the key terms. The idea of negotiating the principle of whether these changes are worthy or desirable rarely becomes an issue, however. But once the principle of change has been established, management have often conceded to shop stewards the opportunity to bargain at the margins on how the changes may be implemented. The extent to which this has been permitted has obviously varied from firm to firm, but management have been acutely aware that the success of initiatives of this type depend on enlisting trade union support and winning over employees' co-operation from the outset. One of the best ways of gaining such support is when management seek trade union agreement, for once accepted it is easier for management to justify the changes to the shop-floor.

There is considerable evidence also that, in instances where management have been forceful in introducing change, even to the point of by-passing and marginalising employee representatives, they have subsequently found the need to develop some form of co-operative alliance with trade unions. This has usually taken a number of forms:

1. *Re-Structuring Trade Union Co-operation*: This form of trade union co-operation is best exemplified by the recent case of organisational change at Cadbury Schweppes', where management's strategy, although intimately bound up with a new assertion in industrial practice, was not divorced from some form of union co-operation. Established institutions like the Works Council were dissolved and the privileges and authority once accorded to shop stewards were resolutely withdrawn. However, in parallel with management's efforts to suppress certain stewards' influence, other more moderate stewards' authority was being actively sponsored. Thus, despite management's efforts to rid itself of an obdurate industrial relations infrastructure, they have not sought to, or wished to, remove trade unions completely from their organisations. There

remains the need to win over employee and union consent for management's goals.

2. *Co-operation at Different Levels*: With this form of co-operation the extent to which management seeks union co-operation varies between different levels of management. In British Rail, for example, in spite of senior management's preference and efforts to reduce union influence over work practices, local management, who lacked the necessary expertise to reconstruct work organisation, needed to call upon trade union representatives to design and implement the changes. As a consequence, the scope for workplace bargaining was considerably enhanced and the influence of shop stewards enhanced.

3. *Tougher in Word than Deed*: The best example of this approach was witnessed in the public sector and in nationalised industries. To be seen to be getting tough with unions, avoiding negotiation and enforcing change by managerial fiat was the overriding priority in an effort to please government paymasters. Many of these campaigns, of course, were led by short-term "macho-managers" who cared little for the industrial relations implications of their actions after their departure. Most commentators agree, however, that the instances of macho-management were rare and that employers' deeds often departed significantly from their rhetoric.

WORLD CLASS MANUFACTURING: A CHALLENGE TO THE TRADITIONAL ROLE OF TRADE UNIONS?

There can be little doubt that the introduction of new forms of work organisation has presented trade unions with fresh challenges. These have taken a number of forms.

1. *Participating in a Dilemma?* Unions face a fundamental dilemma with their involvement in the development of new forms of work organisation: resist and risk marginalisation; concede to agree to management's objectives and invite the rancour of the membership for policing and supporting the implementation of plans which contradict the traditional goals of unionism. Furthermore, while their involvement may strengthen their hand in the short-term, in the longer run their position may be weakened if managers come to

believe that the development of new individual employment practices allows them to operate without unions.

2. *Concession Bargaining*: Where traditionally unions once prized
   themselves on their ability to win annual wage increases, defend
   job boundaries and maintain secure employment for their members
   they are now faced increasingly with the prospect of having to concede these gains in what has come to be termed "concession bargaining". Very often the introduction of new forms of work organisation asks of unions to oversee wage freezes or reductions and
   regulate the terms and rapidity of job losses. A good example here
   is Aer Lingus where the unions are being forced to bargain away
   benefits won in the past.

3. *Repudiation of Collective Bargaining*: Many of the agreements to
   introduce new forms of work organisation are designed to permit to
   management the discretion to manage the organisation of work as
   they see fit. Thus, the paradox of these trade union *agreements* is
   that they often contain clauses which prohibit further negotiations
   over subsequent changes in work practices. Thus, one of the most
   distinctive features of British industrial relations — where the deployment and organisation of the labour force was subject to collective bargaining — has been superseded by the need to accept
   managerial views on what forms of work practices are required.

4. *A Challenge to Collectivism*: The ideology which accompanies
   new forms of work organisation which speaks of team work,
   shared interests and the dismantling of separate divisional loyalties
   and collectivities is often seen to challenge the legitimacy of trade
   unions' independent role in the workplace. In manufacturing, for
   example, craft identification is to be replaced by a team and/or
   product identification. The tensions which such changes give rise
   are further exacerbated where union membership is spread across a
   number of unions. Also, within such teams, team members are
   typically encouraged to approach their supervisor if they have a
   grievance and not their shop steward as they may have done in the
   past. Similarly, the shop steward is replaced by the supervisor as
   the medium of communication of management objectives to the
   shop floor. Here we can see that management are not engaged in a
   direct attack on the existing institutions of employee participation.

These are allowed to remain intact. Rather, it is a case of management going around them, of by-passing the shop steward's organisation and communicating directly with the shop-floor: a "form of temporary derecognition" as it has become known.

5. *More than One Thing at a Time*: Having advocated and called for new forms of work organisation and increased employee involvement for decades, unions are now faced with a managerial strategy which purports to grant employees greater discretion and participation at work. With these new initiatives contradicting avowed managerial strategies of the recent past, trade unionists are understandably suspicious of what they may conceal. Furthermore, and this is particularly the case with total quality management, management have deliberately sought to couch their objectives in a language which trade unionists find difficult to discredit. This problem is particularly evident in the service sector where managerial attempts to introduce new working practices have been systematically tied to the provision of a quality service or product. The problem for trade unions then becomes: "how can such a strategy be resisted legitimately without incurring the managerial charge that unions are solely bent upon undermining the quality of service to the public?" Thus, new work structures represents more than one thing at a time for employee representatives: an expression of hope, promising increased employee participation and job satisfaction, and an increased threat to their role as employee representatives.

6. *A Shift from Occupational Skills to Enterprise-Specific Skills*: In other instances, the threat to trade unions is not posed by new forms of work organisation per se but, more by the new working practices and skill structures which accompany them. Traditionally in British industrial relations, unions have defined their membership around particular occupations, "job territories" and specific technologies. In certain situations, particularly with a number of the craft unions, control over training extended across the national labour market. The establishment of new work structures, however, is often associated with the creation of enterprise-specific skills. Thus, instead of looking for people who possess a single craft skill, employers are more concerned that people develop a portfolio of skills which are congruent with the production needs of the busi-

ness. As individual trade unions increasingly lose control over training so their ability to maintain particular job territories diminishes. No longer, therefore, are modes of job regulation and training mutually reinforcing as they have been in the past. Obviously, however, if management seek only to make marginal changes in work structures they may unwinningly continue to give credence and legitimacy to such job controls. But where change is of a more significant nature, the challenge to trade unions' identity and conventional means of organisation may prove to be substantial.

7. *Lessons from Europe*: Some important lessons can be learnt from Europe. Here the law plays a crucial role. The presence of legal guarantees for trade union organisation and participation in change programmes has helped to foster a more positive approach to restructuring and the introduction of new technology than is generally evident in the UK and Ireland. While these changes may have important industrial relations implications there too, trade unionists can be confident in the belief that issues of competitiveness are the stimulus for their implementation and not a wish to marginalise unions. In general, European companies have introduced new mechanisms of involvement and participation not to undermine existing industrial relations institutions but to operate in parallel and complementarily. It is significant, for instance, that the most extensive introduction of QCs in Europe is in France: hardly a devise to marginalise unions when French unions are perhaps the least effective in Europe. However, in countries where such legal supports are absent is it little wonder that employee representatives should fear the implementation of new work structures.

Before going on to consider some of the key lessons/questions raised in this paper it should be pointed out that the concern thus far has been to focus on the difficulties, disadvantages and the tensions which new forms of work organisation holds for managers, employees and trade unions. This focus has been deliberate: to temper the sometimes naive optimism which one sees in the more prescriptive literature.

KEY LESSONS/QUESTIONS
The following lessons/questions are grouped under individual heads for managers and unions. In many respects this is a false and inappro-

priate division as both parties share similar concerns and problems; it is done for ease of exposition.

For Management

1. In the UK, the common perception in the late 1970s and early 1980s was that manufacturing's lack of competitiveness was due — in large part — to strong, militant trade unions. Other countries were more competitive, it was argued, because it was easier for employers to introduce change in the workplace. This interpretation is now questionable. In comparison to unions in other European countries, the problem for British unions was not that they were too strong but rather that they were, and are, too weak. It has been this weakness which paradoxically has not helped British firms reach world class manufacturing status.

   To an Irish and British audience the suggestion that institutional constraints on managerial freedom may in fact promote the development of world class manufacturing may, at first sight at least, appear counter-intuitive. But companies most likely to adopt such initiatives are those which operate in countries, like Germany and Sweden, where union representation and negotiation rights are ensured by legislation. Unable to pursue the low-wage, low-value-added route for their advantage, these companies are forced to innovate in other ways to overcome the handicap of strong shop floor organisation. The introduction of world class manufacturing systems is therefore necessary to sustain a high wage economy. As paradoxical as it may seem, British unions have been too weak to close off a cheap labour avenue for management, albeit that they have not been helped by recent government legislation which has been aimed at de-regulating the labour market. In Ireland, while de-regulation has not gone as far, there are still considerable opportunities for employers to seek to take the cheap labour route.

2. There is a tendency for employers to see many of these new work organisation techniques as discrete activities with little co-ordination between them and other aspects of personnel and industrial relations practice. In some organisations it is not unusual to have managers in one room doing industrial relations fire-fighting while young MBAs down the corridor are striving to win the hearts and minds of employees.

A number of elements are important here. For example, those employers who have and wish to persist with recruiting a cheap disposable workforce, must ask themselves if this employment strategy, together with their attempts to win employees' co-operation through new forms of work organisation, will convey a unified purpose to its employees. Likewise, security of employment should be a consideration: the New Deal at Rover, for example, was arguably made successful by management's ability to convince employees and shop stewards that the introduction of team working and other new work practices would not lead to widescale job losses.

3. The next lesson follows logically from the above and that is the need for employers to develop strategies for their dealings with trade unions. This may come as something of a surprise, but when employers are asked of this, it is often difficult to identify clear policies towards collective bargaining and unions. Some strategies would appear, on the one hand, to be aimed at developing an individual relationship with employees rendering trade union representatives redundant. On the other hand, however, there are few organisations who actually possess the managerial means to manage employees individually. In terms of resources in people and time such strategies impose severe costs. And, if management seek to narrow the number of items entering a collective bargaining forum, have they developed other means which may be usefully employed to resolve such issues.

   Furthermore, is it possible to reconcile a strategy of seeking to win over employees' commitment when at the same time one is deliberately trying to marginalise their representatives' influence?

   But if employers do not wish to marginalise unions, the question then becomes: can employers develop appropriate policies where their wish to maximise the individual involvement and contribution of employees can be reconciled with employees' desire to remain within a union and have collective representation?

4. For those employers who do wish to invest in new forms of work organisation the following issues will also have to be borne in mind:

a) It will require a considerable investment in training for both employees on the shop-floor and management, which will need to be sustained over a long period.

b) Middle management and supervisors must be intimately involved in its introduction. For not only have they a lot to contribute, but if they were to be omitted, the resulting feelings of resentment and fear for their futures could stifle any extension of employee participation on the shop floor.

c) If workers are to be convinced to relinquish old job classifications and territories in exchange for new work structures with increased participation, then, managers in turn must be trained to facilitate their involvement: any hesitancy to move away from old, authoritarian styles of supervision may shatter employees' expectations. Thus, line management's role in developing new work structures amongst their subordinates must be closely monitored and, where appropriate, rewarded.

d) When new forms of work organisation give rise to productivity improvements, as they are designed to, then the challenge for management is not to be tempted to use the new efficiencies merely to reduce head count but to work towards acquiring new markets for their products. To seek further reductions in staff numbers will inevitably lead to a reduction in staff commitment to the new work structures. Similarly, if such improvements lead to reductions in overtime, have employers developed some means to compensate employees for a loss in earnings?

e) Another important lesson from my own research was where employers introduced new work structures to mask other motives — job losses and increased effort levels — employees' co-operation quickly evaporated. On the other hand, where change was accompanied by an increase in employees' skill levels and levels of autonomy there was a greater degree of co-operation for increased flexibility and change in roles.

In summary, the main question management will have to ask themselves is: how committed are they to a strategy of new forms of work organisation? They must be aware that there are advantages and costs in pursuing such a strategy.

For Trade Unions

1. Notwithstanding the role of the PESP, the decentralisation of collective bargaining in Ireland is an important factor in understanding the relative weakness of Irish trade unionism. Unlike elsewhere in Europe, Irish unions now lack the framework of national multi-employer bargaining to establish and develop standards for entire sectors. This problem is compounded further by the decentralisation of negotiations within organisations. Very often unions lack effective company (as opposed to workplace) organisation. Conversely, employers find it relatively easy to co-ordinate apparently decentralised negotiations.

Similarly, there is great pressure on unions to concede to what has been termed "wildcat co-operation", where representatives agree to accept company initiatives which run counter to national union principles (e.g. abnormal terms of employment for new recruits; use of overtime rather than additional employment). Unions are often forced into such situations in an effort to grapple with decreased bargaining power and adverse economic conditions. This "company egoism" further undermines the cohesion and unity in the union movement.

For unions to develop a proactive response to new management initiatives there needs to be greater effort put into co-ordinating union officers and educating them. The recent Congress report is a step in the right direction here. This, too, can be an aid to management: a well-informed union representative is more likely to react in a calm and constructive manner to proposals for new forms of work organisation than one who lacks such expertise.

It may be worth considering having a combination of bargaining at different levels. In most European countries the growth of company-level agreements have accompanied and not displaced industry-level agreements — so for example, the broad principles of pay, hours, work practices, etc. may be set at a national level, but specific pay and grading systems, organisation of shift patterns, etc. may be left to company agreements. In this way unions can develop a co-ordinated response and employers are left with sufficient room to develop a flexible response to their own specific situations.

2. Above I pointed to the difficulties multi-union structures pose for employee representatives in developing a strategic response to management initiatives. There are "institutional solutions" to this problem, most notably in the form of single table bargaining for both manual and non-manual employees. Moves in this direction have however, been rare, as it usually poses problems for both parties. Unlike other European countries, there continues to be differences in the terms and conditions of employment of the two groups. Management are afraid that it will open a litany of levelling-up demands and unions fear losing their separate identity. If these problems can be overcome I believe the capacity for employees to develop a strategic response is enhanced.

3. In an effort to avoid charges of "concession bargaining", union representatives may wish to enlarge what has heretofore been largely a narrow agenda in collective bargaining — focusing primarily on the wage effort bargain. Could this be extended to wider areas like training and participative forms of work organisation?

8

World Class Manufacturing in a Semi-State Environment: The Case of Bord na Mona

Dr. Edward O'Connor

Managing Director,
Bord na Mona

INTRODUCTION

World Class Manufacturing might be a new name for what we are doing, but it is not a new concept. Since the final dismantling of protectionism in the early 1970s, Irish industry has had to operate at world class level. Once the consumer had access to products or, to a lesser extent, services, from outside this island, he was voting with his cheque book. If the product could be had better, or cheaper, from somewhere else, then the Irish product was pushed aside. Only by offering something better and more innovative could the Irish manufacturer or service supplier survive.

The focus on World Class Manufacturing is increasing. The globalisation of international markets, the advent of the European Single Market and soon the implementation of the Uruguay Round, means that consumers have choices which their parents could only have dreamt of. And it is not just a question of consumer choice in the retail market. It is interesting to watch the major row taking place between the German car manufacturers. The new policy, which has such an impact on Volkswagen and which is being sought by Opel, is the purchasing policy, the way in which a very large manufacturer deals with its suppliers.

IMPLICATIONS FOR IRELAND

For Irish business to compete in this global market, two things matter: innovation and quality, and all that these concepts mean in terms of research and customer focus.

We do not have a great track record of innovation in Ireland. We have not invested sufficiently in R&D; we have not made the constant search for product improvement and development the cornerstone of our commercial base in the way we should have done. Our education system has not fostered a technological bias with science and engineering giving way too often to the humanities. Industry was content to operate on "me too" technology — usually the tried and tested and therefore the least innovative.

This country is fortunate in having one very important asset, which gives it a competitive edge in the world market. We have a young, well-educated and relatively highly-skilled labour force. But it is a labour force which thinks, and has been encouraged to think, in terms of employment, not in terms of work. It has not necessarily been taught to look for opportunities or to take risks. It might be worth pondering on the outturn of the PESP: an 11 per cent per annum increase for the civil service and a 3-4 per cent increase for industry.

Much has changed in the last five or ten years. Innovation is seen to be a fundamental element in the commercial mix. The infrastructure is being restructured to promote more innovation and a greater awareness of quality. The importance of enterprise is beginning to be recognised. We now know that we must encourage the risk-takers, help to nurture new ideas and give young entrepreneurs and innovators the support they need to get started, to put their ideas to work. A business sector which is turning increasingly towards innovation and towards entrepreneurship is turning towards world class manufacturing.

THE BORD NA MONA EXPERIENCE

What are the particular implications of the move towards world class manufacturing for the semi-state sector in Ireland? To a considerable extent the commercial state sector in Ireland is resource-based. For the purpose of analysing the topic of World Class Manufacturing it may be useful to consider the Bord na Mona experience.

Background

The fundamental position of Bord na Mona changed in the 1970s. We had been set up in 1946 with a mandate of developing the country's peat resources. But added to this was a strong, and explicit, social mandate. Together with the ESB, we were the major employer in the midlands — a region which still today is disadvantaged relative to the rest of the country in terms of its industrial base. We employed 4,000 people, plus, another 1,500 or so on a seasonal basis, an aspect which is particularly important in an area of small-scale agriculture. We were more or less typical of the semi-state sector: a job with Bord na Mona was a job for life.

What we did at the beginning was new and exciting — in peat terms. Originally, we were world leaders in peat technology, but this lead was lost because of a reluctance to continue investment in the research and innovation programmes required to stay ahead.

When the price of energy quadrupled in 1973, the result was world-wide recession, from which it could be argued we are still suffering. But it also caused national governments to re-assess their indigenous resources and their strategic energy policies. The result was the Third Development Programme for Bord na Mona, which instructed the company to find new ways of improving productivity and to find new ways of adding value to peat — at that time our only indigenous energy source. This expansion and investment programme was to be funded by borrowing rather than equity.

In 1979, energy prices rocketed once more, reinforcing the prevailing view about the likely future trend of world energy prices and the pressing need to reduce dependence on imported fuels.

But although Bord na Mona was instructed to borrow to pay for the investment programme to meet the new demand for indigenous fuel, price control meant that we were not allowed to increase prices in line with the world rise in energy prices. A conflict arose as to whether we were a commercial entity, making rational investment decisions based on the market return of those investments and the prevailing price of capital, or whether we were an arm of government policy.

Our prices were held low to try to reduce the Consumer Price Index. Because of the cheapness of our peat briquettes, not surprisingly, we could not meet demand. A decision was taken to build two new briquette factories. One of them was built, the other, in spite of substantial expenditure, never saw daylight.

In 1985, energy prices fell by 70 per cent. Then just when we were crippled by debt, and with an extraordinarily high cost base, we had two disastrous summers in 1985 and 1986, with the consequent impact on peat production. It was not possible for Bord na Mona to compete with world energy prices at that time, and we had been prevented from making any return on our enormous investments at a time when energy prices were high.

We were also losing ground in another important market — that for horticultural peat. We lost out comprehensively on price to new entrants into the market. By 1986/87, the position was fairly bad — and our staff knew it. Morale was at an all-time low, and uncertainty was rife.

A change of management occurred in 1987 and we looked at restructuring the company from top to bottom. We had to improve productivity, we had to look at our production technology and, above all, we had to embark on a fairly drastic cost-cutting programme. At that point, we were so uncompetitive that our very survival was in doubt.

We began with the new management structure which was multi-disciplinary and team based. We proposed an extensive redundancy programme. We offered four weeks' pay for every year of service on top of statutory redundancy pay. Two and a half thousand workers were let go under this programme.

This was a painful experience for everybody in Bord na Mona. Morale, internal communications and pride in work all suffered among the remaining workforce. However, there was widespread realisation that this level of surgery was necessary. To preserve 2,200 jobs, a further 2,500 had to go. Aer Lingus later faced similar problems.

We worked together with the unions in putting together and implementing the redundancy programme and had the full support and co-operation of the unions in everything we had to do.

Responses

It was recognised by everyone concerned — management, unions and staff — that cost-cutting through redundancy would not be enough. We had to change our work practices at the same time. We knew that a fundamental restructuring of how we did our business had to be undertaken to create flexibility in adapting to changing markets, to improve productivity and to improve our competitive position. After extensive negotiation, the enterprise scheme was introduced with the full agreement and co-operation of all parties.

The Bord na Mona enterprise scheme allows our staff to form their own autonomous enterprise units, which are team based and where the unit's earnings are directly related to performance and productivity. *Our workers have become their own bosses.*

The spirit of enterprise this has brought into Bord na Mona has increased productivity per worker in a way that is truly amazing. Our productivity has increased by 75 per cent. Our people now make their own decisions and take their own risks. The series of work groups or enterprise units that have been set up have different structures, but essentially Bord na Mona supplies them with services and they produce quality peat, at a price which is agreed in advance. These are people who, formerly, did what they were told to do, got paid whether or not peat was produced, whether the sun shone all summer or whether it rained all the time. They are peat experts — the people who know their own bogs best and know most about their own machines and how to produce peat.

The new work practices and systems we have introduced amount to nothing less than a fundamental restructuring of the organisation. They have maintained in operation our unique skills, maximised the crucial expertise in peat which our employees possess, while at the same time introducing that degree of flexibility which has made us dramatically more competitive.

The new element of profit and risk introduced through the enterprise scheme makes us a fairly untypical semi-state. It also makes us realise the value of our people. They know for themselves the desperate inefficiencies and costs of the old system. By freeing them up to do what they know best — work their own bogs to produce peat — we have motivated them to do it better. We, the management, have taken on ourselves what we know best — planning, distribution, marketing, selling, research and development.

I have no doubt this is the pattern of the future — we are not in conflict with our workforce, we co-operate with them. If you look at the horticultural industry in the Netherlands, one of the most efficient industries in the world, that is exactly how it is structured.

Small, specialised growers do what they know best — produce the product and then they group together in larger forms to create marketing and sales units and R&D units. This gives them the flexibility to change as the pressures of the market demand.

The measures we undertook in a bid to reduce costs and enhance productivity — indeed, effectively to save the company — have turned out to be the kinds of actions which have led us to world class manufacturing. The new enterprise culture within Bord na Mona has itself bred greater motivation and a greater dedication to innovation. For instance, we began to look seriously at the technology we were using.

In the peat business, becoming world class means being as good as, or better than, the Finns. Their technology in peat production, and the generation of electricity from peat, is second to none. Some would call this benchmarking. We did it before we heard the name — we did it to survive, we did it because we wanted to be as good as the best.

With a workforce highly motivated to improve productivity — because now they are running their own businesses which depend on results — we got into technology transfer from Finland and we expanded our own R&D function. We set up the Peat Research Centre. We developed new systems in-house and designed new production equipment and machinery. We became involved with the universities where we sponsored research to help us innovate further. We became a technology-driven company. Productivity went up by 75 per cent.

With innovation very much now becoming the focus of this organisation, we looked to our customer care too. We had always been a production-led company, but now to compete in international markets we had to become market-led.

We decided that divisionalisation was the key to success in becoming market-led. Our businesses are diverse, with radically different factors driving them. For our Peat Energy Division, the production of milled peat is the core business, which is then sold to our main customer, the ESB. Horticulture Division is an international entity which innovates constantly and sells a range of horticultural products to both domestic and commercial users throughout Europe and further afield.

It is an extremely competitive, price-driven industry where again R&D is vital. The Horticulture Division is committed to entering the customers value chain and applying innovation to create further value for the customers there.

The Solid Fuels Division sells primarily to the Irish market of domestic consumers of solid fuels, mainly peat briquettes. But it is also engaged in developing new products and new markets for its products.

The Environmental Products Division (EPD) is in an altogether different end of the business. This is one of the most exciting areas for us. Capitalising on the unique biological properties of peat, our scientists are engaged in developing new products like Puraflo, which is used in water treatment systems, and Biophore, an air purifier which reduces industrial noxious emissions. EPD also offers extensive laboratory services where, using peat-based media, it carries out, for example, soil and water sample testing and monitoring services for a range of clients like county councils, manufacturers and others in Ireland and abroad.

This process of divisionalisation created virtually autonomous businesses which are responsible for their own finances, marketing and other needs and have the freedom to develop the strategies most appropriate to the needs of the market each serves. All are market-led and wholly customer oriented.

Our newly introduced work practices included a comprehensive commitment to improving quality in all areas — in the production and manufacturing process, in our marketing and in our service to customers. Every one of our horticulture factories today has ISO 9000 status and our briquette factories have all been awarded the Q. Mark.

Those are the kinds of fundamental structural changes brought about in Bord na Mona over the past six years or so. All of this has been achieved with hardly a day's industrial stoppage.

Industrial Relations Becomes Human Resource Management

We go on emphasising all of those world class manufacturing ingredients — we celebrate winners in entrepreneurship and enterprise through the Managing Director's Award for outstanding endeavour; we celebrate technological innovations with a special award.

We have a set of corporate values which emphasise the customer, profits, our staff, and above all, innovation. After a long process of participation and studying best practice worldwide, we adopted at board level the value that "it is the right of staff to innovate and the duty of management to facilitate it".

So, by 1993, we have built a new vision for Bord na Mona with our employees — a vision based on innovation. Some of our more recent innovations have included the development of an extremely successful tourist project — the Clonmacnoise and West Offaly Railway — which allows people, many for the first time, to travel by rail out onto a bog. Always aware of the importance of bogs as an eco-system, we lead the way in bog conservation. We work closely with the Wildlife Service of the Office of Public Works in doing that. We look constantly at environmental projects and at ways of preserving and enhancing the cutaway bogs. We have created a new craft industry — Celtic Roots — which uses the oak and yew found on the bog floor to make sculptures.

Despite the difficult summer of 1993, we achieved almost 85 per cent of our peat production target, as against 40 per cent in the last comparable summer of 1985. We are using the latest technology, re-searching new business areas and new products. We have a wholly-owned subsidiary in France and the UK and joint ventures in the Netherlands. We have a technology company — Mona Engineering — which looks constantly at ways of improving peat production and de-velops new machinery. We are hired as consultants in the Baltic States and even in the US. Not only are we competing with the traditional industry leaders — the Finns — we are compared favourably with them, and Bord na Mona is now ranked a world leader in the peat in-dustry.

We are looking to the future with confidence. We have proposed to Government that a new 120 MW peat-fired power station be built. This is a concept we researched and developed. We carried out fea-sibility studies, which were presented to Government. The power sta-tion proposal has now been included in the National Development Plan.

The new power station, as conceived by Bord na Mona, would utilise the latest Finnish technology. It will create 300-350 jobs over its lifetime. It will guarantee a continuing strategy of having an inde-pendent indigenous source of energy which insulates us to some ex-tent from fluctuations in world energy prices.

The existing peat-fired power stations are highly inefficient be-cause their technology is out of date and because they require high manning levels. They are also nearing the end of their useful lives. Peat currently supplies 14 per cent of the national electricity grid.

That's projected to decrease to 10 per cent by the end of the cen-tury as the existing stations are de-commissioned. This will happen in a period when the ESB's own projections forecast an inexorable rising demand for electricity, together with a continuing upward trend in world energy prices to which Ireland will be exposed. National energy policy must dictate that the remaining 130 million tonnes of peat be utilised to meet this situation. We need efficient power generation and we need lower prices for peat. We need an indigenous source of en-ergy. We need to go on innovating and adding value to our natural re-sources — peat, people and land. The new power station we have proposed will fulfil all of these demands.

Why are we proposing this? Because we know that using the latest fluidised bed technology, such a power station can generate electricity at the same level of efficiency as the ESB's flagship power station — Moneypoint. We also know that, by building this power station, which will allow us to add value to 130 million tonnes of peat left on the bogs, we can reduce the price of all peat we supply to the ESB. We can bring down the price of peat far enough to make it wholly competitive with alternative fuel sources. In fact, the price of peat at the moment is very much distorted by the element of subsidy built into it. That subsidy stems from the decisions I talked about earlier — which have left us with a burden of £180 million debt.

We have a strong base now on which we can build but it is critical that the unmanageable part of our debt — the part that is historically related and which arose outside any actions by Bord na Mona — is stripped out. This would also fulfil the demands of the Culliton Report. This restructuring of the historic debt and the building of the new peat fired power station only can confirm the value of all that has been achieved and secure a long term viable future for Bord na Mona — but they make economic sense for this country. We are not talking about a bail-out. We are talking about a strong, successful commercial entity which has transformed itself and is competing profitably in international markets and can continue to grow, develop and add value to a vital national resource.

CONCLUSION

Here I must return to the themes which I began with. How does a company like Bord na Mona, using a natural resource, become and stay world class? The issues are innovation and quality. We must always stay slightly ahead of what our customers want. For us there is a strong focus on R&D. This is and must remain a constant theme. For any company it is a major investment, for a company as cash strapped as Bord na Mona, it is a real issue to find the money to stay ahead. And it is not just a money issue, the management of research and development, the planning of it and for it, places strains on managers which are probably underestimated. Doing research and development is one thing, making sure that the company uses it and responds to it is a real challenge. But it is where Bord na Mona sees its future and we are meeting the challenges posed.

And what else lies ahead for the new Bord na Mona? Our vision into the next century spells out a diversified energy company. We are already involved in Ireland's only substantial alternative energy project — a wind powered project in the west of Ireland. Our aim will be to progress further the alternative energy potential, including wind and biomass projects. Innovation and R&D will clearly play a pivotal role in those developments. And we will go on using our technological strengths to make our horticulture and environmental products businesses into major international enterprises.

We built a vision with our employees. We face strong competitive pressures selling energy and peat products in both the local and international marketplaces. Our vision, however, remains intact. With our staff, we will apply technology to find innovative ways to enhance the value of what we produce to meet our customer's changing needs.

9

World Class Manufacturing: Implications for Work Practices and Employment

Sean Donnelly
Executive Director,
Industrial Development Authority

To create and sustain jobs in the manufacturing sector in Ireland we clearly need the right economic environment in the country and internationally. Companies, for their part, need to pursue the right strategies and, above all else, they need to be competitive.

COMPETITIVE ADVANTAGE IS THE KEY

Competitiveness is and will remain the big issue for Irish industry. If companies lose market share, jobs are inevitably put in jeopardy. This is the case whether we are talking about the many foreign-owned companies we have been attracting here, or indigenous Irish-owned companies. If we are selling Ireland as an industrial location, we have to compete with many other countries in a struggle that is becoming more cut-throat with every month that passes. Equally, if a company based in Ireland, be it Irish or overseas owned, is selling products or services abroad, it does so in an environment that is also becoming increasingly competitive.

But in the world of the 1990s, being competitive is not just a matter of keeping up with the pack. You don't win with a "me too" approach. It is simply not enough any more. To compete effectively, you have to have at least some areas where you are significantly better than the opposition. The challenge facing manufacturing industry in Ireland is to bring about the conditions which will facilitate the transformation of the existing industrial base and, *critically,* lead to sustained job creation.

THE JAPANESE EXPERIENCE

A number of characteristics may be used to describe the Japanese economy: A small fragmented market on the edge of a major land mass; small local companies without the cash resources to afford the high-volume large-scale production plants which their overseas competitors have established as the prerequisite for competitive success; a labour environment which seeks to maximise employment levels. . .

This description of Japan sets out the scenario which forced the Toyota motor company to discover a new system for organising production which made the most of the situation in which Japan found itself after World War II. This system formed the basis for Japan's successful conquest of the international auto industry 20 years later — the World Class Manufacturing system. The Japanese developed these methodologies by identifying the "state of the art" thinkers — Deming at the forefront — adapting their views to meet their own needs and ways of working and accepting that there would be no quick and easy solutions to their problems. Their overnight success took many decades to achieve.

WORLD CLASS MANUFACTURING — FACTORS OF PRODUCTION

A fundamental difference exists between the West and Japan in the way in which factors of production are viewed. Inventory in a JIT system is viewed as a liability — our accountants see it as an asset. In the JIT system quality is based on zero defects while we are scrap-tolerant. Perhaps most important of all, the workforce — a consensus approach replaces "edicts from on high" and a team approach replaces the traditional hierarchy. Japan has already changed the basis for competition by making World Class Manufacturing effectively a necessity rather than a luxury for companies hoping to compete internationally — or even to survive locally.

THE IRISH EXPERIENCE

A number of characteristics may be used to describe the Irish economy: A small open economy on the edge of a major land mass; generally small local companies; overseas subsidiaries facing increasingly tough international competition; major employment issues.

The question which we in Ireland face is whether we can, in an appropriate way, find a means for transforming our own industrial base in as dramatic a fashion, as the Japanese did over that period.

It will not be sufficient — or indeed desirable — for Ireland to attempt to copy what the Japanese have done. We must learn from WCM and adapt it to our own strengths and weaknesses.

Irish companies are already learning this from their customers. And I should emphasise at this point that to date I have talked about WCM only in the context of Japan. This is no longer true. Increasingly companies in North America and Europe have adopted this approach. It is becoming all pervasive.

OVERSEAS COMPANIES IN IRELAND

Over the last 20 years, overseas companies have been a key element in the manufacturing base in Ireland. The worldwide drive towards competitiveness means it is critical that Ireland is efficient and effective and practices World Class Manufacturing. It is worth remembering, too, that in the 1990s we have to have an economy that can compete just to *hold* the overseas projects we already have.

One of the consequences of the integration of Europe is that international companies will have the opportunity to rationalise their European production — inevitability, there will be fewer, bigger, plants. In that scenario it is vital that Ireland is more competitive than other locations so that we win, not lose, in that process. We will be rationalised out, or in, depending on the relative performance of the Irish plant alongside those in other European countries. In this competitive battle for investment, we fight aggressively to get a hearing, we fight aggressively to get on the short list, and then we fight aggressively when it comes down to the wire — the final choice between coming to Ireland and going somewhere else.

When an overseas company closes down here the general perception is that the decision is often based on some illogical decision made by a senior manager in the US or Germany. The reality is that multinationals base their decisions on the hard facts of competitiveness. Overseas companies here face the same competitive factors as Irish industry, both internationally in the corporate structure and on the market place. The key issue which will determine overseas companies' future success in Ireland is competitiveness.

In services, and across the board, we are increasingly honing our strategic edge by going to potential investors with ideas — not waiting for projects to appear on the horizon, but marketing pro-actively. We need to do this because of the intense competition that is now apparent. The other key dimension to our success that will become even more important is our ability to offer high-calibre people.

Although the Irish industrial promotion agencies do offer a package of incentives to incoming investors, increasingly the financial aspect of those incentives simply keeps us in the ball-park: our deal is, broadly speaking, no better than that being offered by all the other places competing for the investment. We have to offer financial incentives, of course, but increasingly, the key factor in the decision is what we in Ireland can offer in the way of people.

We have a young, well-educated workforce which enables us to offer incoming industries — and to enjoy ourselves — a competitive advantage in the value of the input from that workforce. This is recognised in the latest world competitiveness reports, published by the International Institute for Management Development and the World Economic Forum.

High profit margin, low labour content companies will benefit most from the 10 per cent Corporate Tax — for example, the pharmaceutical sector where the quality of product and quality of people are a driving force, not cost. There are instances where the low corporate tax rate can mask relative lack of competitiveness. From an industrial development perspective we must be wary of falling into complacency on cost by virtue of the 10 per cent maximum corporate rate tax. After all the 10 per cent rate is only of benefit if adequate profits are made in the first place.

WORLD CLASS MANUFACTURING IN PRACTICE

Over the past 10 years, Ireland has built up an extensive automotive component industry supplying the European car industry. A local example is a company based in Waterford, Kromberg & Schubert. Because car manufacturers continuously insist on price reductions and because of severe price competitive pressure from Eastern European supply companies — labour costs in Eastern Europe are one-eighth those of Irish companies — the workforce and management realised that if they were not competitive, they might lose market share. The company had to reduce costs and become more efficient and implement World Class Manufacturing.

Another key factor in the attraction of overseas companies here is the sub-supply infrastructure. The development of strong supply linkages between overseas companies and the Irish economy has been a key objective of industrial policy for the last decade. Considerable progress has been made toward this goal through upgrading the performance capabilities of selected sub-supply companies, identifying and developing linkage opportunities and identifying and solving barriers to linkage.

An indicator of the success of the linkage effort to date is that overseas companies now spend almost £1.3 billion per annum in this country on components, raw materials and other sub-supply items in the areas of electronics, engineering, food and healthcare. This represents an increase of almost a third in local sourcing by multinationals since 1983, when local economy expenditure by industry was first measured by the IDA.

Most overseas companies believe that there are considerable opportunities for the further development of linkages. They have noted the emergence of a pool of strong sub supply companies in Ireland and are actively seeking local sub-suppliers. These multinationals have carried out significant work to date to identify high potential sub-suppliers and build up their capabilities.

An example where this has succeeded is in the electronics industry. Apple Computer Ltd. was set up in Cork in 1980 employing 150 in what was primarily an assembly operation. Today Apple has over 950 people employed in a fully integrated manufacturing facility producing the full range of Apple products.

Apple spends over £90 million every year on its 35 local materials suppliers — this represents 50 per cent of Apple's total European expenditure. Most of these suppliers deliver on a Just-in-Time basis to the plant and have recently been connected through Electronic Data Interchange enabling them to be linked into Apple's replenishment programme which operates on a three-day order to deliver basis. This requires top-class supplier standards.

For most multinationals, it is very much in their interest to have a strong capability locally, particularly for items with a relatively high management/administrative requirement and high transport costs, such as packaging, printing, and plastics. JIT, zero inventories, zero defects, short lead times, high flexibility, and most important of all, a much higher level of communication and trust are all becoming key elements in the relationships between sub-suppliers and end-product producers — in other words, World Class Manufacturing. These attributes of manufacturing are greatly facilitated by proximity, and having suppliers locally is becoming increasingly important for overseas firms as a consequence.

IMPLICATIONS FOR IRISH INDUSTRY

Irish industry has had to surmount many crises over the years: entry into the EC; the decimation of the protected sector of industry; the two oil crises of the 1970s; inflation rates of over 20 per cent; prolonged world recession; and, most recently, it has had to come to terms with severe currency instability.

To survive such instability firms need to become survivors — with the financial strength to ride out the lean times and capitalise on the good times; to develop management; to develop new products; to bring these products to new and existing markets.

Unfortunately, we all know that indigenous Irish industry is still not profitable enough. Although average profitability, according to IDA's yearly survey, has been increasing and is now above the levels in the early to mid-1980s — for non-food companies it is running on average at 6 per cent — it is still far too low to provide sufficient funding for sustainable growth. To weather short term financial storms, quite apart from achieving long term growth, these averages must be increased dramatically.

This is not a task with which IDA is traditionally associated. Yet it is what we have been concerned about, in one way or another, for the last decade.

CUSTOMERS' NEEDS ARE CHANGING

When we talk to Irish companies they tell us that their customers needs are changing. They are being asked by their customers for small quantities, greater variety of product, more frequent delivery, and goods supplied at shorter notice. Those companies which can meet these stringent requirements are being rewarded by winning orders. The clothing industry is a good example.

John A. Hickey manufacturers children's clothing in Dublin. His Irish and UK multiple customers are looking for several product lines per season to reflect the rapidly moving fashion trends. Because John Hickey has introduced Quick Response Manufacturing using modular manufacturing he has the flexibility to change his production line quickly and most importantly get the business.

THE ROLE OF THE INDUSTRIAL DEVELOPMENT AGENCY

The role of the IDA is to help firms build and develop their existing strengths and become winners in what has become an extraordinarily volatile environment. Our Company Development Programme was initiated in the early 1980s to help Irish firms put in place a strategy setting out clear goals and targets for where they want to go and how they are going to get there. Over the years we have refined the programme, in particular to include the implementation of strategy.

One critical element of this implementation process is the role of manufacturing strategy and organisation. To this end we have taken a number of initiatives in the area of World Class Manufacturing. For example, we have undertaken seminar series, pilot studies, such as one dealing with the print and packaging sector, in-house training for IDA personnel and work with individual companies. In taking this approach we are conscious that, as stated already, whatever the benefits of WCM it has to be tailored in such a way as to meet the needs and, indeed, the opportunities facing companies at their current stage of development.

IRELAND'S COMPETITIVE ADVANTAGE

It will, I think, be abundantly clear that the competitive advantage for Ireland that I mentioned at the beginning is *the people factor.* The constraints on growth by Irish-owned companies are almost all people-related. The resources that Irish companies lack are mainly know-how and expertise — and that includes technological expertise, through it's certainly not limited to that. The crunch factors will continue to bring overseas companies to Ireland are also people-related. And the crunch factors that will determine whether existing mobile investment will stay here or not also come down to people — the ability of people working in plants in Ireland to out-perform their counterparts in competing countries.

World Class Manufacturing is about empowering the people on the shopfloor. About moving from a functional organisation to one in which many teams are focused on specific customer or product groups. About personnel policies designed to instil a spirit of continuous learning. It is about empowering workers so that every member of staff is transformed into a problem-solver and quality controller. What we need, and what we have the potential to achieve, is better management based on better production methodologies. We must constantly strive towards achieving our competitive edge as a nation.

PART THREE

COMPETITIVENESS AND EMPLOYMENT
IN EUROPE

10

An Overview of Industrial Changes and Developments in Europe

Tony Hubert ·

General Secretary, European Association of
National Productivity Centres, Brussels

The nature of industry and employment have been changing in Europe and the USA over the last century, the last decade and the last year. And in a GATT-prone European Union, with declining internal boundaries, change in the future will certainly not be slower. In the following, I shall try to illustrate the most relevant aspects of the present labour-management relations scene in Europe under five broad headings: (1) Employment and industrial rationalisation; (2) The relocation of industry; (3) Employment: quantity or quality? (4) The impact on State monopolies and services; (5) Conflictual or consensual labour relations? Each topic is introduced by a relevant example.

EMPLOYMENT AND RATIONALISATION

In 1914 the coal industry in Britain employed one million workers (one-tenth of the country's workforce), and its 3,000 mines produced half Europe's and one-fifth of the world's coal. In 1984, the Coal Board's 170 deep mines employed 175,000 men. In 1994, British Coal's 17 pits employ less than 11,000 men, somewhat more than the private sector mines which had been sold off. In the meantime, the total number of British people at work has increased — notably miners' wives.

Agriculture and Fisheries

Agriculture and fisheries have continued to fall in numbers employed, particularly rapidly in the Mediterranean. Primary sector employment is still declining in the UK, despite its being at the lowest relative level in the world. This employment decline is likely to continue for a variety of reasons.

In the first place, there is the continuing replacement of man by machinery, the prototypical approach to "rationalisation". Output is continuing to increase despite falling labour inputs thanks to better machinery and fertilisers.

Secondly, there is the cost of the Common Agricultural Policy (and the extra expenses that European consumers thereby incur for paying more for Caribbean and Cretan bananas): given all the other demands on it, the European Union's budget will surely not be able to afford such unnecessary expenditure.

A third, related, reason is the necessity for Western Europe to become more integrated with both other European countries (central and eastern) and other parts of the world (notably the USA with its huge economic power), thereby reducing agricultural employment in Europe.

Farmers and farm labourers made redundant have been mainly absorbed, indirectly or directly, in *services* (rather than manufacturing industry, as used to be the case). Or they have become unemployed. So, according to the European Union's corporatist logic, rather than subsidise those working on the farm for being idle, why not subsidise their produce for export? That their subsidised products have driven unsubsidised, cheap central European farmers out of their traditional ex-Communist bloc markets or impoverished African peasants, is hardly considered. In other words, Europe's non-rationalisation often makes non-Europeans redundant, and non-European farmers do not have EU countries' welfare safety nets to fall back on.

Manufacturing

A similar rationalisation process has been seen in the manufacturing industry. The previous decline in manufacturing employment has continued. Even in the USA there have been only slight absolute upswings in employment with continuing relative declines in "old" industries (steel, textiles, etc.) and "new" ones (such as aircraft and computers). Restructuring is a long-standing continuous process (it goes back at least to Gutenberg and printing). One early part of corporate restructuring has been automating repetitive manual tasks. This has continued notably because of high labour costs; and restructuring will continue to make unskilled and semi-skilled workers redundant in all industries, including high tech.

So it is not just in the numbers involved, but also in its nature that manufacturing has changed. With the emphasis on *quality* and *time management* (automotive productivity is now measured in "hours to produce"), advanced industry has come to use more the brains and experience of those who also bring their brawn and hands to work.

The powerful drives which are under way in industry as well as private services focus on *team-working*: TQM, just-in-time, etc., in small, semi-autonomous units which are taking over from large, bureaucratic organisations. When termed "quality circles", team-working was rejected by trade unions; nowadays trade unions actively work for it since all sides agree that it has the best chances of counteracting the shortcomings of "Taylorism" (though Taylorism is actively supported by many workers).

Team-working is closely linked with developing a *corporate culture*, an accepted set of norms about behaviour within the company to which all can adhere. All these approaches have the considerable advantage that they require considerable amounts of *training,* both broad and technical in character. So training and, more importantly, *learning* become part of the culture.

And to work adequately, the involvement and participation generated have to be rewarded by appropriate *financial participation* (though recent research questions whether individualised approaches really do act as incentives).

Even when all such participative approaches operate smoothly, there is still a need for constantly revising structures around changing processes (corporate *re-engineering*), to adapt the totality to the changing (often rapidly) market place. Job security is a chimera, and unions are increasingly demanding *employment security*, which is also, however, a virtual impossibility given the revolutionary nature of change in competition.

Employers and unions make increasing use of the battery of government measures available to smoothen change. Some, like *early retirements*, are extremely expensive for the state, which is nowadays increasingly demanding phased early retirement during which skills can be passed on to younger workers; whereas *training* remains inappropriate for the bulk of an ageing workforce.

Services

Manufacturing's decline has been accompanied by *services'* boom. As US experience since the mid-1980s shows (a continuing boom in exports, both high and low tech), there is no longer any visible connection between the number of "real" jobs, i.e. those producing saleable goods, and the wealth of the nation.

In the west, the universal decline in manufacturing jobs also raises the question of *definitions*. Until the 1960s, many of the jobs which are today classified as "services" were then integrated within "manufacturing" companies. In the meantime, all larger companies, as well as dynamic medium and small companies, have begun *restructuring*, i.e. become "leaner and meaner".

Differing from the past, the restructuring process has often made skilled specialists, professionals, engineers and managers redundant. Some can sell back their skills to their old companies, but as "external consultants". They can also, sometimes with government backing, set up entirely on their own. But as "consultants" they are statistically defined as being in the "service sector".

Executives and managers freely move between industries and consulting — and, despite rationalisations, there is a growing number of the "managers". In fact, a "job" is a better criterion for work rather than "sector/industry": truck-driving can be as monotonous as packaging, assembly-line working or preparing hamburgers, all in different sectors.

These developments raise at least two questions:

1. First, is not the amount of work available relatively finite? If so, attention should be focused at least as much on *work-sharing* as on work creation. This is currently a major thrust in labour relations in several countries, particularly Denmark and France.

2. Secondly, can continuous, *life-long training and learning* even hope to play any significant role? Some argue that this is only possible for those with a broad theoretical and lengthy education, with a strong theoretical foundation.

RELOCATION OF INDUSTRY

The Belgian government passed the "Law to safeguard competitiveness" in 1989. Five indicators were agreed to as showing whether competitiveness was improving, worsening or stagnant: (1) export performance; (2) labour costs; (3) financial costs; (4) energy costs, and
(5) "structural determinants" (i.e. investments, research and development expenditure, etc.).

In 1993, employers and trade unionists agreed that the deterioration of exports and labour costs — notably because of the appreciation of the Belgian franc — was damaging competitiveness to the extent that the three other indicators could not remedy. But they could *not* agree, as also laid down by the law, on advising the government on the measures to be taken. So the government acted, first trying to bring in a "social pact" (refused by the trade unions), then with unilateral decisions aimed at boosting employment and cutting social security expenditure.

In 1994, the social partners are, again, agreed that Belgium's competitiveness is threatened, but again, disagree entirely on what should be done: "nothing", according to the unions, because the previous measures have not had time to work out; "reduce labour cost", say the employers, feeling the impact of German collective agreements of Spring 1994.

In the meantime, Belgium's largest "enterprise" by far remains the national unemployment benefits' agency which "employs", or at least pays benefits to, one million out of a total population of 10 million.

The competition, which is having a negative impact on Belgian industrial relations and on European employment more generally, is coming from all directions. The 1985 Single European Act provided for free movement of capital, citizens, services and goods. All "freedoms" should have been fully in place throughout the 12 countries by January 1993; they are not completely so, and in the meantime, the world has changed even more.

Recent International and Competitive Changes

1. The movement *eastwards* of "traditional" enterprises across European borders is explained by price for relative skills and quality of goods and services, ranging from cheap and dirty manufacturing to cheap and dirty prostitution. The movement is unlikely to be too extensive because of poor productivity and work in central/eastern Europe — good machinery and skills are needed — and political stability is lacking. Good performance will take a decade to achieve. However, the area is not homogeneous, and the queue of potential European Union applicants is growing.

2. The most serious challenge to traditional European manufacturing undoubtedly comes from *Asia*. This is not just from Japan and the

"tiger economies", which are increasingly setting up in Europe, bringing in their own systems of labour relations, but also from the "second-rankers in Asia": Thailand, Malaysia, Indonesia, the Philippines and India, which are competing on cost, notably in high skills' areas (Indonesia produces aircraft). As serious a challenge to goods is that to *services* from these populous and increasingly well-educated south-east Asian economies. Through information technology, they can service European service and manufacturing companies overnight (airlines, insurances, etc.).

3. *Westwards:* The USA exerts a strong pull as a manufacturing location, particularly because of the scale of the market, the competitiveness of US wage rates, the enticements offered by the various states, entry to NAFTA and political stability.

4. *Southwards:* Industry and services have few incentives to move into the Mediterranean economies because of their poor productivity, and hence poor labour relations, record and the different business ethics practised.

5. *Centre-wards:* 75 per cent of the exports of European Union countries are to other member states. Their economies are increasingly intertwined — as, increasingly, are their labour relations through the European social charter. No country can opt out in reality though fewer countries, compared with 1992, are keen on establishing more Euro-procedures, such as European works councils.

But so far, it is the differences between the structure of labour-management relations, rather than any similarities, which are most striking. Re-structured companies are perhaps leading the way for tomorrow's standard employment relations: part-time work, teleworking, etc. And in these enterprises, unions are frequently absent.

The Impact

Pulling the threads relating to location together, the globalisation of business has had a variety of impacts on labour relations:

1. Most obviously, it has put considerable pressure on wage rates and, depending on the country, non-wage labour costs. The reactions of different groups, which have been translated into different policies, have ranged from "keep cheap foreign goods out" of the Union, the

country or even the region through "reduce wages to keep competitive" and "pay subsidies for non-wage costs of unskilled workers", to "let competitive forces play their role". Competitive pressure has been one of the main influences on the negotiation of collective agreements in Germany. The engineering industry lost more than 600,000 jobs in 1992 and 1993. The agreement of March 1994 provides for pay rises under the level of inflation and foresees greater worker flexibility as regards working time and income. This has been followed by similar agreement by the public sector union (ÖTV).

2. American approaches to collective bargaining are being broached in Europe: concession bargaining, two-tier bargaining, etc. These are means for significantly reducing the costs of labour. Single union companies have emerged outside Germany; unions have rethought their own structures (there is a movement in Scandinavia towards consolidation in cartels each covering a single sector of society); and employers' associations are reviewing their role in advanced industrial societies — for instance, the Swedish SAF has withdrawn from co-decision-making in some 50 state agencies, and rationalised itself, reducing its workforce by 37 per cent.

3. Greater emphasis is being placed on "time management": time to design, to produce and to market products to be in advance of competitors. This is achieved notably by reducing enterprises to their core functions, "outsourcing" the production of components to (cheaper) satellite enterprises and using "just-in-time" delivery. Particularly important is that machine operating time is maximised, requiring new patterns of work. This includes an extension of shift work. It can also lead governments to rescind existing legislation (e.g. on night work for women).

4. New forms of labour relations have been brought in, imported through inward investment or adapted by local companies, characterised by slogans such as "flat hierarchies", "employee empowerment", and "lean management". All emphasise using the brains and initiative of the workforce, both as individuals and groups. Several countries have not sought foreign investments notably because of concern for foreign influences, some having subsequently done a U-turn (e.g. France) when the advantages are reconsidered.

5. "Atypical work" is becoming more typical and "typical" work
   rarer. So employment contracts are increasingly likely to be of
   limited duration or of less than whatever the current standard
   working week is or linked to a specific geographical location.

EMPLOYMENT: QUANTITY OR QUALITY?

In the USA, the numbers employed by the top Fortune 500 companies
declined between 1989 and 1992 from 16 million to just over 11 million. In the decade to 1992, GE alone shrank from some 400,000 to
220,000 employees, mainly working in self-managing teams, whereas
its revenues doubled from $27 billion to $60 billion. In the same period, the real incomes of America's bottom quarter of workers fell by
at least 10 per cent.

In the single month of February 1994, US employment grew by
460,000 persons, of whom 12,000 were in manufacturing and three-
quarters were part-time. In the 15 years to 1990, the countries of the
European Union created some 10 million jobs, virtually all in the
public sector.

European countries lack entrepreneurial dynamism: far fewer jobs
all round have been created compared with the USA and Japan. The
private sector in particular has a poor track record, and the bulk of
new jobs have been *part-time*. In as far as it depends on public finance, the employment situation can only deteriorate in the future
since most EU states have limited money for job creation (which in
the end means additional taxes).

Developments on the different sides of the have given rise to the
debate: do we want jobs at any price or "good" jobs? Compared with
the USA, European job-holders have maintained their incomes,
though at various reduced rates for the unemployed depending on the
country in question. At the present time, European countries are split
into groups of "haves" and have-nots, with trade unions representing
the "haves".

Added to this is the continuing continental European debate on
"Taylorism": the division of labour and the workforce into those who
think, decide and supervise and those who do. The lesson of the past
decade has probably been that managerially-led, evolutionary innovations in "human resources management", particularly under pressure
from competition, have had a far greater positive impact on work than
quantum leaps like Saab-Scania, Volvo-Uddevalla and Saturn, USA.

The European Union (cf. *White Paper on Growth, Competitiveness and Employment*) currently sees seven avenues along which partial answers to the problem of unemployment might be found:

1. Providing better and more employment-relevant education and training systems, which will not, however, *create* any jobs.

2. Increasing flexibility in the labour market and in companies.

3. Introducing more profitable procedures at the company level for re-organising work.

4. Reducing indirect costs of targeted semi-skilled and unskilled workers.

5. Making better use of public funds earmarked to fight unemployment — they are usually passively handed out as benefits.

6. Specific actions for poorly educated young people.

7. Finding new types of unskilled and semi-skilled employment — tapping the black market for jobs.

STATE MONOPOLIES AND SERVICES

The largest employer in Germany between 1990 and 1993 was the Treuhand Anstalt. This typical official agency of the "social market economy", where government has traditionally splashed out large subsidies to smoothen industrial decline, has managed, and subsequently sold off, more or less, the whole of East Germany's labour force of roughly 8 million people.

Now that its function is virtually completed, it is notable only because of the scale of its top managers' salaries. And this in a country where the official hourly cost of a worker in the engineering industry is some DM42, which compares with a Belarus working illegally at his side for DM5.

State monopolies and services exist for different reasons:

* Some were created because they were "natural monopolies".

* Others were rescues for ailing private industries.

- Still others were created by nationalising private companies for reasons of ideology.

- Still others to stimulate development in a backward region, etc.

In some countries, at least, they have been useful channels for "jobs for the boys". All these basic reasons have been questioned in the 16 EU countries over the last decade or more. Moreover, state monopolies are likely to run counter to European law and can only continue to exist in the shorter term. So what is the current situation?

Although all European Union economies say that they are moving towards privatisation (free competition is required by the Treaty of Maastricht) or "corporatisation" (restructuring existing monopolies to operate like a private enterprise), the speed and political climates differ: from virtually a standstill in Greece, to a little in Italy and Spain, momentum-with-hiccups in France and Benelux, to a broad or radical extent in UK.

Trade unions have been extremely reticent about allowing governments to privatise national monopolies, let alone services relating to health care, cleansing, law enforcement, etc. But there is a growing realisation that the current ethos focuses on the individual, rather than the mass, and that it *is* possible to distinguish between policy determination and monitoring, on the one hand, and programme implementation, on the other. Moreover, companies with money are better bargaining partners than public authorities without.

Privatisation can, moreover, help fill government deficits (those currently under way in European industrialised countries are estimated to be worth $2,000 billion). But where countries have used public corporations as "jobs-for-the-boys", there is a powerful lobby not to change. Few arguments are heard nowadays about selling the family silver.

Telecoms have led the way. But there are still as many telecommunications operators in Europe which are public as there are privatised. Once privatisation has taken place, it is rarely the current wage-earners who suffer, but the potential new ones, who do not have a job. And industries or companies which have "inappropriate" demographic profiles are shown by experience to lack competitiveness.

What is a state monopoly in one country, or region, is not necessarily so in another. With a borderless Europe, state monopolies are confronted with both private and public enterprise from other states. For instance, public or private telecommunications or employment services (or parts thereof) can set up legally in another state and "trade" there. Since employment services are generally very large and bureaucratic, several governments are passing legislation to de-monopolise or allow private enterprise in.

Once privatisation is accepted as not necessarily being the worst form of life, service and quality become key issues, just as in other enterprises: the service exists for the client, rather than to provide the producer with income.

CONFLICTUAL OR CONSENSUAL LABOUR RELATIONS

After decades of conflictual industrial relations, the Port of Rotterdam Authority established, jointly with the social partners, the Platform for Innovation and Technology in 1985. The concept was that in a booming sector on which perhaps some 150,000 depended, directly or indirectly, for their income, it would be more appropriate to foresee problems and try to resolve them in advance rather than have an in-dustrial free-for-all about dividing up the existing cake.

In the meantime, competition has become more severe; Antwerp is a mere 50 miles distant, Hamburg hardly more distant from the indus-trial heartlands of Europe. The size of the unskilled labour force has significantly declined, but the demand for skilled labour has in-creased. However, those living in the immediate employment area of the Port are overwhelmingly from groups who rarely fully complete their basic education, notably non-white Dutch. Under these circum-stances, the Port Authority is trying to work out how the Port should go about harnessing technological and economic change which would otherwise detract it from being the best port in the world.

Though not necessarily typical, this example is symptomatic of changes in labour relations taking place in Europe.

First, "cheap" industries can no longer be maintained in Europe: coal, steel, footware, basic textiles, etc. Yet the political pressure is there to maintain existing jobs at almost any price. Witness the con-troversies over the hullabaloo of the intended closing of 30 British mines in 1993 or the move of Hoover from France to Scotland. An important strand in labour relations has been to devise means to help redundant workers start new lives, such as by becoming self-employed.

Secondly, collective bargaining is increasingly addressing the question of job maintenance or "employment security". Those collec-tive agreements so far devised, notably the 1993 Volkswagen agreement, trade off security for short-time working systems financed by society, with less than proportionate decreases in wages. Extensive recourse to these could rapidly bankrupt the state. On the other hand, an agreement like this also emphasises the importance of using the "non-working time" in which workers should be trained in the new technologies of car manufacturing.

Rotterdam tries to look, as a collectivity, at problems proactively and seize opportunities before others even perceive them. But it is constantly faced with traditional attitudes and skills' gaps. And, indeed, with the drive by those who live within its "employment basin" to want to acquire the skills in question, notably because of the small incentive to work compared with welfare benefit.

Thirdly, jobs in the future are likely to be either relatively low-skilled and low status (stevedores, janitors, paramedics, etc.) or high skilled in higher value-added industries (crane operators, pilots, etc.). In as far as more people are required to have higher skills, the change can be painful and contested by traditional blue-collar workers who want continuing subsidies, and some intellectuals, who want (for others) "work-sharing". Three countries — Britain, Denmark and Holland — have the largest extent of work-sharing in the European Union, through part-time work, which is currently being negotiated elsewhere (Germany and France).

Fourthly, unions have become more wary about using the strike as a policy instrument. Transshipments can be diverted "temporarily" to Antwerp, only to stay there "permanently". The overall level of unionisation has fallen as blue-collars have been replaced by "white-blouses" and collars and services have taken over from manufacturing as the main employers. At the same time, companies throughout the world have become more mobile and "outsourced".

Fifthly, then, with the change in labour force there has been a changing agenda of demands. On the one hand, it is no longer the union which demands and the employers who react: the "reverse thrust" means that previous achievements have to be prioritised, particularly to enable jobs to be maintained, if not created through joint negotiations. And projecting current wage developments into the future, it could even be conceivable that US situations could be achieved — gradual wage declines; trading off wage levels agianst growing numbers of jobs, albeit of poorer quality.

Sixthly, areas of joint agreements and actions are being negotiated. Of paramount importance is training and education. Whereas employers in some countries, such as Sweden, refuse unions the right to co-decide on the use of training and development funds — a function purely of corporate policy, they claim — elsewhere (e.g. Norway) there is a flourishing co-operation council deciding how best to link such training to unions' and managers' concepts of "corporate development".

However, it is not just in the collective bargaining area that labour relations are changing. In particular, government almost everywhere is developing its own agenda through social or socio-economic pacts, through programmes associating both sides of industry or through its own measures aimed at propagating forms of "atypical" work. Prime among these are part-time work, various types of fixed-term work contracts, training leave, etc. Government needs resolution in the face of resistance to change. Witness, for example, French youth reactions to reducing minimum wages, with which trade unions have become associated.

There are few examples of converting semi-skilled or unskilled workers to skilled (Leroy Somer), and still fewer of medium-term successes. Like co-operatives, they appear to be doomed in a capitalist society. Why? Perhaps the lack of basic training cannot be compensated for.

CONCLUSIONS

The unskilled are basically those who are most under threat in the present and future systems. Their situation will be exacerbated by the borderless Europe, with extensive amounts of cheap "foreign" labour, often illegal, flowing in. An important question is whether the welfare state can let their standards of living decline to any significant extent, as in the US model, or whether it can afford not to.

Equally under threat are the medium and highly educated young people, even when their studies are very relevant to the enterprise. For most they are too expensive for their likely yield in the shorter term. And currently companies tend to think shorter term.

The highly skilled, a declining proportion of the labour-force, will have a better lot, but will have to invest more in continuous training and learning.

Finally, trade unions and, *ipso facto*, employer bodies will spend more time and effort restructuring and re-determining what their basic missions are.

11

The European Union and Developments in Industrial Relations

Phillip Beaumont[1]
Department of Social and Economic Research,
University of Glasgow

INTRODUCTION

My basic task in this paper is to try and offer some insights into the likely impact of EU directives on the industrial relations systems of the various countries concerned. In order to try to reach the stage of being able to put forward some forecasts and predictions I will present some material under five basic headings: (1) The Lessons of History; (2) The Industrial Relations Debate; (3) Seeking to Predict Impact; (4) Activities Across National Boundaries? and (5) Some Practical Illustrations. In what follows, these various headings and items will be discussed in turn.

THE LESSONS OF HISTORY

The basic question of concern here is simply: What do we actually know at the present stage, on the basis of previous historical experience? In my view there are at least three important points to note here.

The first point I would make is that trade unions always have had a "tough time" in highly competitive product market settings. This is because of the difficulty that they face in trying to "take wages out of competition" in such circumstances. The clear lesson across the long haul of history in many countries is that highly competitive product market settings are associated with (a) relatively low levels of union organisation and (b) highly centralised collective bargaining arrangements. At the present time it is clear that unions are seeking (in keeping with the lessons of history) a centralised approach, although this will obviously be difficult to achieve given, firstly, that national boundaries have to be crossed and, secondly, that the predominant trend (favoured by employers) in individual systems is towards decentralised decision-making processes.

The second lesson is that of the 1980s and early 1990s, namely that the major impact on industrial relations arrangements at the level of the individual organisation came indirectly from non-industrial relations specific influences. That is, it was developments in the product market (increased competition, shorter product life cycles, changing customer demands) and in the capital market (increased short run financial pressures) that were associated with attempts to reformulate the nature of competitive strategies, internal corporate restructuring, increased mergers/take-overs etc. that really drove changes in industrial relations in these years. This particular observation/lesson in fact leads to my first prediction, namely:

1. The increased integration of product and financial markets in the EU will have greater impact (albeit indirectly) on industrial relations arrangements than will any EU directives directly concerned with industrial relations.

The third point is that historically the industrial relations structures and practices of the EU countries vary substantially. That is, there are important differences in matters such as the extent of union organisation (12 per cent in France to 73 per cent in Denmark), the level at which collective bargaining is conducted, the role of works councils (underpinned by legislation in Belgium, France, Germany, Spain, Portugal, Luxembourg and the Netherlands), the tradition of legal regulation in industrial relations (particularly strong in Germany and France), etc. This being said, there were certain pronounced industrial relations trends across Europe in the 1980s, notably the following (Ferner and Hyman, 1992):

- employers seeking greater flexibility and decentralisation of decision-making;

- weaker union movements, variously involving lower levels of union organisation and less inter-union co-operation/co-ordination;

- government initiatives to deregulate the labour market and tighter control of public expenditure;

- a weakening of "corporatist" (highly centralised, tripartite) industrial relations arrangements; and,

- a reduced overall level of strike activity.

The strength of such trends should not, however, be exaggerated, as most commentators still emphasise the diversity, rather than convergence, of industrial relations systems and labour market arrangements in Europe (see Figure 1).

THE INDUSTRIAL RELATIONS DEBATES

In talking about the social dimension of Europe and directives concerning information, equality, participation and employment standards it is important to identify the key points of debate, not to say controversy, which have been involved in the process. In essence the following issues/debates can be identified.

1. Is it desirable and possible to have a European model of industrial relations? The pro-case (largely associated with Germany) involved considerable reference to the notion of "social dumping". That is, it was necessary to seek harmonisation to avoid a flight of capital to the low labour cost southern European countries. The counter to this argument was essentially two-fold. First, it was alleged that the problem of "social dumping" can be exaggerated as the low labour cost countries are also low productivity ones, have relatively under-developed infrastructures etc. And secondly, the practicality of aspiring to a European model was questioned, given the strong, historically grounded differences in industrial relations between countries.

2. The second question was to do with exactly what sort of European model was appropriate? (Rhodes, 1992). This debate involved two sub-themes, particularly (but not exclusively) played out between the UK and Germany. First, did centralised or decentralised systems of industrial relations perform best in the sense of helping to produce both relatively low levels of inflation and unemployment (i.e. macro-level performance)? And secondly, how should labour flexibility, particularly given the movement towards a more fixed exchange rate regime, at the level of the individual organisation be brought about (i.e. micro-level performance)? Should it be a high wage/high productivity model emphasising quality, training etc. which was stimulated by rigidities in the external labour market (the West German approach)? Or should it be a low labour cost approach characterised by the deregulation of the external labour market (the UK approach)?

FIGURE 1:
LABOUR MARKET TRENDS AND THE IMPLEMENTATION OF DIRECTIVES

Labour Market Trends in the 1980s

- Over the 1980s, average hours worked fell in all member states, but the UK. This reduction averaged 4 per cent in the years 1983-91, but reached 13 per cent in the Netherlands (NB: hours fell predominantly where they were already relatively low).

- In 1990, Germany's labour costs were the highest in Europe, being 15 per cent higher than in Belgium (the next highest) and nearly six times than in Portugal. Labour costs in the Netherlands, France, Denmark, Luxembourg and Italy were within 15 per cent of those of Belgium. However, variations in labour costs per unit of output were relatively small due to large differences in productivity.

- Over 70 per cent of the German and Danish workforces have completed post-compulsory education/training courses compared with 30 per cent in Spain and 15 per cent in Portugal.

- In 1965-91, the number of women in employment in the EC rose by over 13 million, while the number of men fell by 1 million.

- During the 1980s, employment protection legislation was weakened in France, Portugal and the UK, but strengthened in Italy and Spain. Perceived constraints (from protective regulations) by employers were greatest in Italy and least in the UK.

The Implementation of Directives

At the end of 1992 the implementation of directives (33 applicable) in the social and employment fields was as follows: Belgium (70 per cent), Denmark (91 per cent), France (82 per cent), Germany (68 per cent), Greece (70 per cent), Ireland (91 per cent), Italy (64 per cent), Luxembourg (61 per cent), Netherlands (70 per cent), Portugal (73 per cent), Spain (70 per cent), UK (97 per cent).[*]

---

[*] Notification of implementing measures is not always the same as genuine application of EC law (at the end of 1992 Belgium, France, Greece, Italy and the UK were all adjudged to have failed to comply with judgements in the social field).

3. What is the best route to achieve this model? Should it be via directives becoming enshrined in national-level legislation (favoured by Germany and France with their strong legal traditions in industrial relations) or does collective bargaining between the "social partners" have an important role to play?

What seems fairly clear is that the notion of harmonisation centring around a single model (the German one) has receded over time. The principle of "subsidiarity" and the shape of the works council directive (and indeed all the various proposed employee participation directives) particularly seem to indicate an increased recognition of (a) the relevance/importance of acknowledging differing industrial relations traditions/practices and (b) the potential role of collective bargaining as an alternative to directives via national legislation.[2] At the same time, however, delays in the process have occurred, new developments have taken place (e.g. proposals to increase membership of the community, the opening up of Eastern Europe, the emergence of new sources of low wage competition in Asia), and many (legal and non-legal) uncertainties remain. For example:

1. Will the social partners at the European level take the opportunity to use collective bargaining as an alternative to directives via national legislation?

2. Is the collective bargaining route without problems? What if collective bargains are not legally enforceable? Can the results of collective bargaining be extended to the growing non-union sector? Can the collective bargaining route be satisfactorily monitored to ensure adequate compliance? Do the European level bodies (i.e. ETUC and UNICE) have the mandate and legal basis for producing effective framework agreements?

Despite these sorts of uncertainties and questions, what is clear to practitioners at the individual organisational level is that EU employment directives will be forthcoming (and indeed have been[3]) via some combination of national legislation and collective bargaining. The question then becomes, what is their likely impact? The question of impact has two basic dimensions: (a) how extensively will (the content of) the directives be adopted/implemented (see Figure 1) and extended throughout national industrial relations systems[4], and (2) will the impact of the directives on balance be viewed as a "constructive source" of change.[5] It is only the first dimension of this change process which we can meaningfully discuss at this stage.

SEEKING TO PREDICT IMPACT

The whole industrial relations field is littered with the bodies of brave individuals who have sought to predict and forecast developments, only to see these predictions quickly undermined by subsequent events. So I am very conscious of stepping into something of a "lions den" in this regard. However, let me suggest that the impact of EU industrial relations directives will vary considerably between different countries, with the greatest degree of adoption/implementation and impact coming about in countries characterised by (a) a relatively receptive industrial relations environment and (b) a system with the characteristics most likely to spread and diffuse the essence of these directives.

The first question posed by this observation is, what exactly do I mean by a *relatively receptive* industrial relations environment? The first defining condition that I would adopt here is that the substance of the directive should be relatively consistent with on-going trends and practices in the industrial relations system. In contrast, the least receptive environment will be where the substance of the directive strongly diverges from on-going trends and practices. Let me illustrate this proposition with a simple example. In the UK the procedures for joint consultation over redundancies (which very much derived from a European directive in the mid-1970s) have in practice not worked as envisaged due to the strength of the off-setting lump sum compensation approach established by national legislation ten years previously.

My second defining condition concerns the notion of "best practice" which has typically informed the nature of national industrial relations legislation. In essence, most countries have taken the position that best practice enshrined in national employment law is what the better employers have been doing for some years on a voluntary basis and that now it is time to try and bring (via legislation) the rest of employers "up to speed". However, if the notion of what constitutes best practice varies (as seems likely) between countries at any point in time, then EU directives will receive a relatively receptive response in national systems where there is relatively little difference between the nation of best practice in the directive and in the national system concerned. Again a simple example to illustrate the proposition. French multinational companies have been very much to the forefront in establishing information sharing and consultation bodies with unions across their various operations simply because this practice fits fairly closely with their national level legislation (i.e. the 1982 Auroux legislation providing for national group-level committees).

To summarise, the implementation and impact of EU industrial relations directives will be most apparent in national systems with a receptive industrial relations environment, which involves the essence of the directive fitting reasonably well with on-going trends in the system, and embodying a notion of best practice that does not overly stretch the notion of best practice in the national systems concerned.

The second stage of the process is that the impact of the directive will be greatest in industrial relations systems characterised by an above average ability to spread and diffuse the practices and standards embodied in such directives. What does such an industrial relations system look like? The results of various cross-country studies suggest that the systems with the most capacity and capability in this regard are relatively centralised ones, systems characterised by considerable internal cohesion in the larger (e.g. confederation) union and management representative bodies, and systems where there is a tradition of relatively co-operative union-management relationships.

The importance of these sorts of influences seems to be borne out in a recent study by our colleagues at the European Foundation for the Improvement of Living and Working Conditions (EFILWC, 1993). In essence they found that the degree of employee involvement in the introduction of new technology was as listed in Figure 2.

Although not a perfect fit (no model ever is!) the rankings observed in Figure 2 seem to accord reasonably well with the previously listed features. That is, with the features of a national industrial relations system that produce an above average ability to diffuse "best practice" throughout the system as a whole.

To date I have, at least implicitly, been suggesting that the implementation and impact of EU directives is likely to vary between countries, and I have sought to offer a possible explanation for any observed variation. However, is there any channel or mechanism that can reduce the extent of this variation, and thus be something of a source of convergence between countries? The most obvious candidate is the multinational (MNC) or transnational corporation. As we have seen in so many European countries (Ireland, the UK, Spain, etc.) it is the MNC which frequently constitutes the spearhead or lead sector in industrial relations change (moreover the changes which they are spearheading are frequently similar across national systems), which then becomes something of a role model for others to emulate. Furthermore, it is a fairly safe bet (one of the few in this subject area!) that MNCs will be among the first to implement EU directives if only because of their visibility, sizeable internal resources and the fact that some of the directives are specifically targeted at them.

FIGURE 2:
THE EXTENT OF EMPLOYEE INVOLVEMENT IN THE INTRODUCTION
OF NEW TECHNOLOGY

	Planning Stage	*Implementation Stage*
1. Top rank	Denmark, Germany	Denmark, Germany
2. Middle rank	Ireland, Netherlands, Belgium	Ireland, Netherlands, UK, Greece, France, Spain
3. Lowest rank	UK, France, Spain, Greece, Luxembourg, Portugal, Italy	Portugal, Italy, Luxembourg

Source: (EFILWC, 1993)

The likelihood of MNCs being to the forefront in implementing EU directives is likely to be particularly so in the case of MNCs adopting a European-wide approach to industrial relations matters. Those MNCs most likely to fall into this category have been viewed as likely to have the following characteristics (Marginson, 1992): (a) a single ownership and management structure within Europe and (b) they produce similar products/services in different countries for integrated production across national boundaries.

In short, not all MNCs are the same. But the above point to the particular type of MNC which is most likely to take a European-wide view of industrial relations matters. Such a perspective is likely to initially translate into the establishment of management-only consultation arrangements (see Figure 3) and arguably then management-union consultation arrangements. However, whether the latter will then evolve into a third stage, namely union-management negotiation/bargaining arrangements seems much more problematical. I will return to this below.

FIGURE 3:
RESPONDING TO THE EUROPEAN WORKS COUNCIL
DRAFT DIRECTIVE: A MAJOR EUROPEAN
MULTINATIONAL CORPORATION

1)   This well known MNC has more than 12,000 employees in its key production centres in the UK, France, Germany and Spain.

2)   The existing industrial relations arrangements in these locations are highly diverse in nature; a works council in its major German plant, 2 of its 3 plants in France are non-union, its major UK production location has a single recognition agreement, while in Spain a multi-union situation exists.

3)   From the mid-1980s a European human resource management co-ordinating committee has existed. This body, which meets 4 times per year and involves the leading management HRM specialists in the UK, France, Germany and Spain, has traditionally concentrated on identifying individuals with high management development potential, and then rotating them on job assignments to match business needs. More recently the committee has sought to harmonise certain terms and conditions of employment (e.g. pensions) in individual countries and across Europe.

4)   Some 18 months ago a sub-committee was established to examine the draft directive on European works councils. The sub-committee adopted the following initial stance:

   •   No company initiative would be forthcoming until the directive was clarified.

   •   Any consultative, information sharing arrangements between management and employee representatives must not become a joint negotiating/bargaining body.

5)   The sub-committee have responded to the appropriate bodies in individual countries and at the European level concerning the draft directive, and are much happier with the nature of the present draft than was the case with the original draft.

ACTIVITIES ACROSS NATIONAL BOUNDARIES?

Earlier I argued that competitive product market environments have always posed difficulties for unions and that their response has been to seek to develop more centralised industrial relations arrangements to try and take wages out of competition.

There are a number of levels of union activity that can be usefully identified; although discussed separately here, it is likely that they will overlap to a considerable extent and indeed mutually influence each other. The most obvious starting point is the exchange of information between the unions themselves across national boundaries. There is a relatively long-standing tradition of such activity (albeit somewhat *ad hoc* in nature) in dealing with MNCs and undoubtedly this will increase (and indeed has) as a result of the integrated market developments. Indeed the Commission has made available funds (over 1992 and 1993, some £24 million) to facilitate transitional meetings of worker representatives from European MNCs. This funding appears to have widened the sectoral basis of such meetings/arrangements beyond the well-known cases of metal working and chemicals. Moreover they have assisted the establishment of European Industry Committees — the sectoral federations of unions affiliated to the ETUC — which many commentators expect to play an increasingly important role in "European industrial relations".

A second level of potential activity is that the contents of the social charter may increasingly influence the bargaining agenda of individual unions in individual countries. In the UK a good deal of media attention has focused on the GMB agreement with Keiper Recaro (a German car seat manufacturer) in the early 1990s which incorporated provisions of the charter, including the establishment of a works council, at their Birmingham plant. But this still remains a very atypical example in the UK. It is also relevant to note here that the working time reduction campaigns orchestrated by engineering unions in Germany and the UK (and Italy) have displayed certain features in common, which constitute something of a "pattern bargaining" approach.

The third level of activity involves the establishment of cross-national boundary consultative and information sharing bodies. Many MNCs have established management-only arrangements along these lines, but what is clear is that more and more employee representative-management bodies along these lines are being established (with, as noted earlier, French MNCs being particularly prominent in this regard). However, what is also clear is that (a) informal arrangements predominate over formal ones, at least in a numerical sense, and (b) management is keen to ensure that these remain consultative, rather than negotiating, bodies (see Figure 3). Indeed the Multinational Business Forum has strongly emphasised that consultation/information sharing with employee representatives does (and should) occur via direct (as well as indirect) routes (a view perhaps not uninfluential in the recent re-wording of the draft directive).

Finally, what about European level framework agreements between the social partners, as an alternative to implementing directives via national level legislation? Currently the ETUC is exhibiting some sort of frustration with the pace of developments (or the lack of them!) in this area. Moreover, larger questions still remain about both the desirability and feasibility of this as a route to implementation (see comments earlier).

SOME PRACTICAL ILLUSTRATIONS

It is only by looking at the issue of practical application that we can ultimately hope to assess the second dimension of impact noted earlier, namely have the directives been a constructive source of change? (This is particularly important to ask of management, given some of their initial reservations).[6]

Firstly, let us take the issue of equal pay, which was a principle enshrined in the Treaty of Rome and was the subject of a European directive in 1975. A recent study of this issue produced the following findings (Rubery, 1992). In 1985, female to male earnings ratios for full-time manual employees were 83 in Italy, 73 in Germany and 69 in the UK. In 1985, female to male earnings ratios for full-time non-manual employees were 69 in Italy, 66 in Germany and 54 in the UK.

Why this divergence? The answer appeared to lie in the strength of different national systems of pay determination (in potentially complementing or offsetting the directives), with the more centralised pay determination systems of Germany and Italy being an important factor in the relative narrowing of differentials. (The earlier observations made about the strength of relatively centralised industrial relations systems in diffusing change should be recalled here.) The above figures may be viewed as an illustration of the inherent limits of convergence within Europe via the directives route. Alternatively, one might want to argue that the extent of convergence without the directives would have been much less.

FIGURE 4:
RESPONDING TO THE EUROPEAN UNION
HEALTH AND SAFETY DIRECTIVES:
A PAPER MILL

- In response to the H&S directives that came into law in the UK in 1993, a temporary task force was established. It consisted of the personnel, production and engineering directors, plus the safety officer.

- With no generic guidelines forthcoming from local area H&S groups, the task force sought to (1) identify priorities and (2) assign resources.

- As a relatively new plant (less than 10 years old) their priority con-centration was on manual handling, personal protection, and the management of H&S.

- The resource commitment involved one of the union-appointed safety representatives working full-time (a "safety technician") for 15 months to carry out risk assessment exercises. As a back-up, three other individuals worked on the exercise on a part-basis for 2 months or so (full-time equivalent). In short the resource commit-ment involved something like 2 man-years.

- The organisation used the occasion of the directives to re-emphasise commitment to H&S, in particular trying to break down the view that H&S was essentially the province of the specialists (i.e. the safety officer). The dialogue between the safety technician and the individual operatives (rather than with supervisors) was seen as being of central importance here.

- The "safety technician" has now trained all of the other union safety representatives to carry out risk assessment work, and this is now an integral part of their work.

- The inspectorate are seeking to use the plant as a role model in the local area. A number of bench-marking visits along these lines have occurred.

What about the response to, and impact of, some of the more recent health and safety directives? In conducting some research in the subject area in the UK recently one of the most noticeable responses I observed was that the directives raised the priority (admittedly with varying degrees of enthusiasm) that management attached to health and safety. In one large service sector organisation that I worked with, this took the form of the appointment for the first time of a full-time safety manager. A more common response was the establishment of a senior management (only) health and safety committee, either for an indefinite or finite period of time. The contents of Figure 4 report one such initiative in a paper mill. In essence the personnel director was of the view: "I would certainly not have sought out such regulations and they certainly involved a considerable expenditure of resources, but there is no question that we have been able to use them to our advantage in raising the profile of health and safety and spreading commitment to it". I suspect that such pragmatic sentiments are not unique to this particular plant. Moreover, the widespread existence of such sentiments will be important to ensure that directives are given the opportunity to constitute a positive source of change over time.

CONCLUSIONS

My predictions/forecasts may be listed as follows:

First, the indirect effects on industrial relations of increased product and financial market competition in Europe will be greater than the direct effects of the industrial relations directives.

Second, the adoption and impact of the directives will vary substantially between countries, with most effect being in industrial relations systems which are relatively receptive in nature and with a high diffusion capability. (The relatively centralised systems will be to the forefront in this regard.)

Third, MNCs will be an important potential counterweight to variation between systems, although this role will not be true of all MNCs.

Fourth, the combination of the first predicted trends means that a European model of industrial relations is unlikely, but that more in the way of blocs or sub-groups of related systems may result over time.

Fifth, the existence of a reasonably pragmatic management attitude at the individual organisation level (see Figure 4) will be an important determinant of whether industrial relations directives come to be viewed as relatively constructive in nature over the course of time.

Footnotes

[1] I am grateful to Mark Carley, editor of the *European Industrial Relations Review*, for a number of helpful discussions.

[2] The latest version has actually dropped the term "European Works Council" and instead refers to information and consultation procedures, structures and mechanisms.

[3] By 1990 when the number of H&S directives had risen to 21 it was estimated that some 75 per cent of UK legislation was the result of European directives.

[4] An important sub-question here is whether the Commission views the implementation process as meeting (their) defined standards (see Figure 1).

[5] The obvious question here is whether both social partners see the changes as being constructive in nature (i.e. constructive from whose standpoint?).

[6] In the UK a recent study of some 45 organisations reported that personnel managers in the main viewed the EC employee involvement/participation proposals as likely to be relatively neutral in impact (on matters such as costs, employment, productivity, employee relations, job satisfaction); 51-70 per cent fell into the neutral category.

12

Competitiveness and Employment in Europe: The European Union White Paper

Padraig Flynn
European Commissioner for Social Affairs

INTRODUCTION

This paper considers the recent European Union White Paper on Growth, Competitiveness and Employment. The issues represented by the White Paper deserve full examination. Great change is upon us, and the role of the Social Partners will be of major importance in determining Europe's success in the 21st Century.

The White Paper is basically a handbook for the management of change and it is a handbook which recognises that change has to have at its core the objectives of sustaining and ensuring growth and competitiveness. Otherwise we will not, in any sustained way, address our unemployment problems. Europe's major problem is, of course, unemployment. This is the central theme of the White Paper. But it cannot be addressed in isolation from the equally crucial issues of growth and competitiveness. If we are not competitive, there will be no wealth creation to pay for the social progress we need. Without growth there can be no return to full employment.

GROWTH

Firstly, in tackling unemployment we need growth. Since 1990, GDP growth in the community has fallen from around 3.5 per cent to minus 0.5 per cent a year, and we must reverse this trend if we are to begin to create new jobs. However, unless we undertake major structural reform, unemployment will not fall by anywhere near as much as it should, even when we get growth.

We have seen this clearly in the Irish context. With economic growth of 2.5 per cent or 3 per cent we will create some jobs. But not enough jobs to tackle the unemployment problem in a lasting and meaningful way. Ireland — happily — does have strong output growth. The 4 per cent the Government predicted for 1994 seems well within reach. But Ireland's average annual growth over the last six years — of 4.7 per cent — has translated into only 0.8 per cent employment growth.

We need to alter the relationship between economic growth, employment growth and unemployment, so as to increase the number of jobs we get from our economic growth — the employment-intensity of that growth. This, colleagues, is not only a key challenge for governments, it is a key challenge for the social partners.

COMPETITIVENESS

Secondly, we have the problem of competitiveness. At present, Europe has real strengths. Our global balance of trade is positive. We have 6 per cent of the world's population but we produce 30 per cent of the world's wealth. The number of European Union plus European Fair Trade Association (EFTA) companies in the top 200 group by turnover has risen in the last eight years.

There is, however, a worrying longer term perspective when we look at changes in global markets, at how we engage and harness new industries, how we develop our competitive strength in-depth, and how we sustain and build our wealth creation — which is so crucial to our social progress objectives. But staying competitive will not in itself solve the employment problem either and, unfortunately, the term competitiveness has acquired in some circles an unhelpful ideological connotation.

Competitiveness is not coded language for wage reduction. It is not synonymous with deregulation or with turning the clock back. It is rather looking to the new settings, work patterns, and labour force composition we need, whereby workers *want to change*, to keep jobs in the long-term as well as the short-term. We must remain competitive but we will not do so by trying to drive wage levels or living standards down to those of our rivals in the developing world. Instead we must renew our capacity to stay one step ahead of the competition, and help ensure that the world economy grows, to the benefit of us all.

Again, it is how the Social Partners perceive and address some complex choices which will decide how competitive we remain and become — how we progress the social and economic agenda hand in hand. We do not, of course, have a God-given right to our present standard of living. Europe has to earn its way in the world like every other region. If we believe that high social standards are important — and I believe we do — then we must continue to generate the wealth needed to pay for them. This is an issue at the heart of the debate: How do we build a competitive European economy for the 21st Century with low unemployment and high level of social protection?

THE EMPLOYMENT PROBLEM

Unemployment is now over 11 per cent in Europe. But we must also recognise the scale of the employment problem in Europe. Only 60 per cent of people of working age are in work in Europe — with Ireland near the average — compared to over 70 per cent in the US and Japan. That is why additional job creation does so little to reduce unemployment.

In the last period of great employment growth, the second half of the 1980s, some 10 million new jobs were created, but only three million of these jobs went to people who were unemployed — the rest went to new entrants to the labour market. And the direct costs of unemployment are staggering. It cost Germany 40 billion ECUs to keep people employed in 1993. Across the whole Community the bill in 1993 was more than 200 billion ECUs. This equates to the GDP of Belgium. It is unsustainable. It is not the foundation of a competitive economy.

The scale of the task is clearly shown by the fact that we need at least 15 million extra jobs if we want to cut unemployment by half by the end of the century. This shows starkly that patching and pasting our systems will not be equal to that task. The issue is not only the employment creation target. The issue is what levels, what kinds of unemployment we think our societies can live with.

If we think we can live with varying levels of the status quo, then we do not need to embark on a fundamental examination of our systems, and the way they impact on the potential for sustaining and creating employment. If we believe that we cannot live with the status quo — whether for political, social or economic reasons — then we must proceed to the development of a medium-term employment strategy based on rebalancing our economic and social policies. The basic objective has to be to change the way our economies and societies work so that we can create more jobs, and improve the Community's overall competitive performance. Again, the quality and honesty of the social dialogue process will be crucial to our chances of achieving that rebalancing.

CHOICES

So, what are the main directions and choices which the White Paper suggests? The medium to long term answer is clear: We need a radical shift in the nature of our education and training systems in order to ensure that our workforces are adequately equipped to take on the new jobs, harness the developing technologies and make them productive for Europe. This means starting at the beginning in primary school and also a major investment in the ongoing training of the existing workforce. Of course, this must be done in partnership with industry, but the scale of the challenge leads me to believe that government money will be necessary. There is perhaps a case for the issue to be integral to collective bargaining.

In the short term we must find creative ways of helping the unemployed back into the labour market which encourages them to improve their skills and which respect their dignity. We must do all that we can to fight against the emergence of a deprived underclass. Specifically, we need to:

- improve the flexibility of the labour market

- actively examine new ways of combining earned income and income support

- reduce the cost to employers of hiring the less-skilled

- make a major effort to help our young people to get a start in life by offering them a guarantee that all young people under the age of 20 will be given the chance to either be in full-time education, or in a job, or in some form of work-based training.

This implies a major shift away from passive income support towards pro-active employment policies of the kind pioneered in Scandinavia. There is no simple or single answer. The solution will come from a series of measures whose cumulative impact will help us to move forward. The White Paper offers a number of options from which individual countries must choose.

WHITE PAPER PROCESS

I can't address here all the ideas, possibilities and challenges offered by the White Paper. But I would urge those interested to look carefully at Chapter 8 of the document, my particular contribution to the process, which I believe offers a thoughtful and balanced agenda for the employment dimension of our task. The follow-up work is being energetically pursued in Member States and in the Commission. I am looking in particular to the deployment of structural funds to our objectives — in terms of young people, the long-term unemployed, reskilling workers, and urban problems — to name only a few.

NEW CONVENTIONAL WISDOM

Last Spring, early in this process, the message I took to the Social Affairs Council was that we had to look anew at all our processes and mechanisms. That employment should no longer be an accidental winner or loser in the design and implementation of government policies, across the board. Since then we can at least claim that a new conventional wisdom is emerging in Europe, and across the OECD area, which reinforces this view. It is reflected in changing concerns in the United States. It is reflected in the Brussels Council conclusions. The new conventional wisdom recognises that our problems are multi-dimensional. There is a new awareness that we need a careful balancing of choices. That most policies have negative as well as positive effects. We need to look at how to achieve this balance, in the name of social and economic progress.

Perhaps we need to *re-invent government* to respond to the challenge, to move away from our present *tramline approach* to decision-making. Perhaps it is *not only the workplace* which has to transform itself. Perhaps we need to *recreate* or, in large company parlance, *re-engineer* our structures and government for the 21st Century too.

I am delighted that the White Paper policy proposals reflect so closely the priorities of the Irish Government. I was pleased by the fact that the thrust of the last budget was almost exclusively that of employment growth. I note also the wide range of measures aimed at boosting business and enterprise, and their particular focus on the small and medium sized enterprise which is crucial to our objectives. And I was pleased at the emphasis given to human resources in the Irish National Plan.

The wide range of measures and the careful targeting of these measures which we are discussing with the Irish authorities will en-

sure that the priorities set out in the White Paper are effectively addressed. I am pleased that the measures will address not only the most
urgent needs of industry but also the long-term development of human
resources in Ireland with a particular focus on those who face the
greatest barriers in seeking to enter the labour market. And I am very
pleased to report positive and constructive discussions with the Social
Partners during my visit to discuss the White Paper follow-up.

While the White Paper is only a framework, it is, I believe, a very
useful and important framework. But in the end, it will be up to each
Member State and particularly governments and social partners to find
their own formula for making the necessary changes.

The choices we now face regarding how the labour market works,
how human resources are equipped and how wealth and jobs are distributed are what will decide the shape of employment and unemployment in the future Ireland and Europe. There's a long way to go,
but we have started to move in the right directions. We must press on
together — across the negotiating table — within Ireland and across
the European Union.

13

Competitiveness and Employment:
An Employer Perspective

John Dunne
Director General,
Irish Business and Employers Confederation

THE WHITE PAPER'S MESSAGES AND PROPOSALS

The first message in the European Union White Paper on Competitiveness and Employment is that the Union needs to increase its growth rate by at least 3 per cent per annum up to the year 2000. The paper also sketches out some of the main pre-conditions: a higher rate of investment (24 per cent of GNP instead of the current level of 19 per cent), an increase in saving, stability of macro economic policies and attention to rebuilding confidence.

Secondly, the White Paper emphasises a need to put the accent on medium and longer term measures to improve competitiveness.

Thirdly, the paper highlights a need for greater job content in growth. For 17 years the community has had a similar rate of economic growth to the United States, but the United States has created millions more jobs.

Some of the White Paper's proposals for dealing with the problems are worth noting. They include the creation of an environment more favourable to enterprise within the internal market including a dedicated programme for small and medium sized enterprises. They put an increased emphasis on growth — proposing, for example, an adjustment in the legal framework so that those willing to work shorter hours do not lose out on social protection and conditions of service; improving the prospects for entry into the labour market by making it possible for social security to top up income from work with appropriate safeguards; and by launching a new Youth Start Guarantee programme. It is estimated that significant employment potential exists in the local services area; in the Audio Visual Industry and in environment-related investments.

HOW COMPETITIVE IS EUROPE?

A key issue, in terms of estimating the degree of future adjustment necessary is "how competitive is Europe today". Let's start with a definition of competitiveness. It is the ability of a firm on a sustainable basis to satisfy the needs of its customers more effectively than its competitors by supplying goods and services more efficiently in terms of price and non price factors.

By most indicators the relative competitive position of the European economy has deteriorated progressively over the last 20 years.

Annual growth in employment creation was a very modest 0.4 per cent in the last 20 years, a fraction of the achievement of other Organisation for European Co-operation and Development (OECD) countries. A noticeable feature of the analysis is the fact that new jobs in Europe were generated more in the state sector than in private enterprise.

The European Union's share of the world trade has declined in volume and in value terms at a faster rate than its competitors especially the high performing Asian economies. The share of total inward Foreign Direct Investment (FDI) into the Union has declined. The EU's share of total inward FDI to all OECD countries fell from 60 per cent to 40 per cent between the 1970s and the 1980s.

There are a number of factors leading to the decline in competitiveness. Chief among these is that the unit labour cost of production manufacturing has increased vis-à-vis competitor economies. For example, hourly earnings in the Union group are nearly twice the rate of those in Japan and the US. Other contributory factors are the higher rate of inflation in Europe (it averaged 5.7 per cent between 1982 and 1992 compared with 4.1 per cent in the US and 1.8 per cent in Japan); the lower profitability of capital invested (the US Department of Commerce now reckons that the annual rate of return in Asia is over 23 per cent, twice the EU average); private sector investment is only half that in the high performing Asian economies, and European industry has been slower to adapt to new industrial technologies than its competitors.

Technology improvement and innovation will be a key requirement in the future. Europe has spent significantly less on Research and Development than either Japan or the US at some 2 per cent of Gross

Domestic Product compared to 3 per cent. For example, there are three times as many scientists employed in industry in the US than in the EU The level of co-operation between firms and universities and between firms themselves is also less effective in the EU than in Japan and the US. From an Irish perspective the situation is even more critical. Growth expenditure on Research and Development in Ireland was estimated at £234 million in 1991. As a proportion of Gross Domestic Product, it has increased from .73 per cent in 1981 to .91 per cent in 1990. Whilst this represents a degree of relative development, the sad fact is that Ireland still lags behind the majority of other member states.

A particular issue which appears problematic relates to Europe's demographic profile. The average age of the population will rise imposing an increasing burden on the productive sector. If present policies remain unchanged, governments will have problems financing the extra level of expenditure. More emphasis (and resources) will be placed on finding solutions to the environmental problems of the Continent. With the effective free movement of capital, inward investment decisions will be influenced increasingly by global economic factors.

In looking at Europe's competitiveness, the role of the state is a key issue. The level of state intervention in Europe has increased so much in recent decades that it now represents a drag on economic efficiency through the sheer size of the resources required to finance it.

Expressed as a percentage of GDP, public expenditure averages nearly 50 per cent in Europe compared to 37 per cent in the US and only 32 per cent in Japan. It is also more biased towards consumption, transfer payments to individuals and subsidies to companies. In addition, Europe has consistently run higher budget deficits in the public sector than in Japan or in the US. The large share of public employment absorbs resources, hence the number of people supported by the market economy in Europe is twice that of Japan and one and a half times that of the US. Public investment represents less than 6 per cent of total government expenditure in Europe compared with more than 16 per cent in Japan.

The result is a substantially higher average level of taxation in Europe than in Japan and the US. This high level of taxation and its structure continues to impose higher costs on firms, higher prices on consumers and contributes to higher wages as a consequence. If we keep going in the present direction, even more significantly than heretofore.

For all these reasons, European business is calling for a major reduction in the size of public sector spending and therefore in the level of taxation necessary to finance it. It also calls for a reduction in the number of unnecessary regulations, the number of tasks undertaken by the public sector, and a continued reduction of state aids. It seeks a transfer of available resources towards investment expenditure in the key areas of education, innovation and productive infrastructure, improvement in the productivity/efficiency of those activities that remain in the public sector, and finally the provision of incentives to increase savings targeted at productive investment in the small- and medium-sized sector.

WHAT NEEDS TO BE DONE

Labour Costs

By far the dominant factor of total added value is labour costs, counting for upwards of 60 per cent. Thus it is disturbing to find that in Europe hourly labour costs in manufacturing were 23 per cent higher in 1992 than in the United States, while a decade ago they were 30 per cent lower. Apart from the exchange rate difference more expensive social security systems in Europe are a significant component of these differences. Labour costs in the EU are nearly five times as high as in Asia and Eastern Europe. The argument is however, *not* about reducing labour costs to this level: What is suggested is that the route to better remunerated employment will be through higher productivity, i.e. jobs filled by workers with higher skills. I must hasten to add that this does not mean in the interim that we jettison the lower paid jobs in labour intensive lower technology industries. It is absolutely vital that we continue to adopt policies and take actions which will support these jobs, and also to realise that there will always be sectors where levels of technology, skill, and the intensity of labour costs are such that the relative level of pay cannot be higher. Failure to take appropriate policy decisions in this context will simply result in a worsening of the employment situations.

Capital

Looking at the provision of capital we can ask some pertinent questions. Japan has the lowest real after tax cost of capital followed by the US. Why is this? Both economies have lower interest rates, larger stock markets, and more preferable tax treatment for investors. Europe needs to emulate these conditions, in particular to get interest rates down, and to initiate more favourable tax treatment, especially to facilitate investment in R&D and provide easier access to capital.

Productivity

Expressed in terms of value added per hour, manufacturing productivity in the European Union shows a gap of at least 10 per cent between the major member states and Japan, and at least 20 per cent with the US. Europe does not lead any of the top nine sectors of industry. We need higher levels of investment, more labour market flexibility, better developed infrastructure and improved manager performance if we are to improve Europe's position.

Labour Market Flexibility

Contributory causes for Europe's relatively poor performance compared to more competitive nations include the tax wedge (resulting in a lack of incentive to rejoin the labour force), a shorter working week, weak labour mobility, costly redundancy provisions, narrow wage differentials and weaknesses in the level of education and training. Flexibility of employment must be increased. Among the things required are new work contracts, including part-time work, the greater use of fixed-term contracts and temporary work.

Entrepreneurship

It has been found that the pace of restructuring in the manufacturing sector in Europe is slower because of the low-risk propensity of managers, dependency on state subsidies (which slows down the pace of change), the high cost of redundancy (which discourages hiring), substantial environmental changes, and a tax system which is not friendly to small firm development.

Profitability

European companies do not, generally speaking, make as much money as their American or Japanese counterparts. Why is this? Many of the inhibitions to the profitable expansion of business mentioned above have not been tackled at political level. Certain actions could help. For instance, ensuring that wage increases do not fully absorb the growth of productivity, improving the productivity of working capital and providing the cheapest possible source of finance to small firms.

IMPLICATIONS FOR IRELAND

At the national level, there is a clear need for the adoption of policies which support and develop enterprises so that they are able to compete in the world market. In the industrial relations context we know that pay is a key factor. We also know that pay is determined in different ways throughout the European Union. Some countries operate almost exclusively at enterprise level, others at sector level, others via a combination of national, sectoral and enterprise interests. Each country will have to decide for itself what is the most appropriate means of pay determination.

Outside Ireland there is some evidence of an orientation more towards the level of enterprise because of the increasing globalisation of competition, which is impacting even on the strongest of industries within the strongest of countries. More and more this will require an acceptance of continuous change, improvement and flexibility, and as a consequence of this an emphasis on the level of performance of groups and individuals at enterprise and employment level. For this reason, it seems certain that while pay determination may require a national forum and a national consensus, and perhaps nationally negotiated arrangements, it will almost certainly also require an increasing enterprise and employment dimension.

Turning to the domestic economy the issue of how public service pay is determined continues to be crucial. Not in the sense of whether increases are arrived at through central arrangements but in terms of ensuring that the reforms explicitly provided for in the PCW are actually implemented. The outcome of these changes must be to ensure that the public service pay bill does not increase in a way which is damaging to the competitive position of enterprises and employments based in the Irish market, but competing at home and abroad with foreign-based competitors.

I am talking here particularly about the conciliation and arbitration scheme which up to now has operated in a way and with a criteria quite unrelated to the ability to pay and/or the performance of the employer or the employees within its various sections and departments.

THE ENTERPRISE AND EMPLOYMENT LEVEL

For all employees their employment is going to be subject to continuous change. There will be ongoing issues for a continuous improvement in the level of performance so as to ensure that they will survive and develop. In future this will require a major commitment to communication by employers. The challenge to persuade employees that more flexible work practices are part of ensuring the survival of the enterprise should not be underestimated and will require management capability and innovation of a high order.

The future will also require a less interventionist position on the part of employer organisations and trade unions. This has already happened to a significant degree in respect of employer organisations. The role which they play vis-à-vis their members is now very much that of a professional, advisory and representative organisation rather than one based on defensive protectionist bargaining, maintaining the lowest common denominator for groups of employers combining for this purpose. For trade unions, a move in this direction will mean a greater acceptance of the development of a direct relationship between management and employees in the enterprise. If the development of business and enterprise is to be based on better and fuller communication, an attitude of problem solving and a commitment to non-disruption, then a concomitant requirement will be that third party agencies and institutions such as the Labour Relations Commission and the Labour Court will be required to perform at a highly professional level of competence.

CONCLUSION

It is clear that the challenges of competitiveness and employment in Europe require a series of actions — and fresh approaches. Governments must persuade their citizens that their future is best served by change and that to protect the future, attitudes to work must be made more flexible than heretofore. They must pursue policies designed to reduce their involvement in the economy; and by this process enable resources to be directed towards increasing investment, reducing the cost of employment, increasing the return from and incentive to work — and by these means increasing economic growth and employment. They must cut regulation and reduce bureaucracy without dismantling the social framework which is part of our European culture. Managements will need to operate the fullest systems of communication and appropriate consultation, an attitude of problem solving and a preparedness to settle disputes if at all possible within the environment of the enterprise. Employer organisations will need increasingly to assist the development of these relationships and trade unions will hopefully redefine their role so as to operate as professional third party representatives. Finally we will continue to need third party dispute-settling agencies professionally staffed and trained to deal with disputes which cannot be resolved within the enterprise environment and which require highly skilled mediation, conciliation and arbitration.

Europe has shown itself to be economically resilient in the past and I have no doubt will continue to be so in the future, but the challenge is significant and urgent. It simply cannot go on losing its competitive position as it has done in recent years and expect to be able to continue with its traditional standards and support systems.

Ireland, too, has proved itself resilient but has a penchant for not making the most of its opportunities. The next few years will be crucial for this country also. We must ensure that the promised rise in our economic fortunes are used in the most productive manner possible. This means using the increased growth to deal with the issues which have been a constraint in the past. Less government, not more! Reducing the cost of employment, improving the incentive to invest and the returns from investment. Seeing profit as an unambiguously good thing. Embracing change. Being moderate in our expectations for income development. Continuing to work on education and skills development. Openness in communication and in confronting problems as they arise. Seeing problem solving on a mutual interest basis as the key to the future. These are the ingredients that will maximise the opportunities in Irish society, because they will maximise the increase in our national wealth and allow us to continue with our traditions of caring for those in need to the maximum extent possible.

14

Competitiveness and Employment in Europe:
A Trade Union Perspective

Peter Cassells
General Secretary,
Irish Congress of Trade Unions

The publication of the European Union Green Paper on Social Policy and the White Paper on Growth, Competitiveness and Employment should be welcomed for several reasons.

First, they make job creation and tackling unemployment the central priority for the European Union for the rest of this decade, with a target to reduce unemployment in the Community to 5 per cent by the year 2000.

Second, they contain specific proposals for investment in the infrastructure of the future, in telecommunications, electricity, railways and gas. The modernisation of these services will of course have industrial relations implications.

Third, they broaden the debate on economic policy including industrial relations policy, from the narrow confines of deregulation and cutting wage costs to the wider and interlinked issues of growth, competitiveness, innovation and positive flexibility.

Fourth, they endorse the European model of development (though recognising that it requires renewal and adjustment) which is based on social as well as economic progress and a high level of social protection for workers and seeks to compete with the best in the world through high productivity, high levels of quality and high standards.

DOES IT MATTER WHICH MODEL OF DEVELOPMENT WE ADOPT?

The former President of the European Commission, Jacques Delors, described the White Paper and the Green Paper as a framework for reflection on the need to modernise and adjust the European model of economic and social development, including the level of social protection and our industrial relations system.

Some may see the question of which model to follow in Europe as a bit theoretical. I believe, however, that the debate being generated by the White Paper on the nature of a competitive model for the European economy is crucial for Ireland.

Some economists are advising governments and companies to compete with China, South-East Asia and Eastern Europe by creating jobs based on low wages, fewer constraints on the dismissal of workers and lower standards of social protection. This advice is being given at a time when the new US administration, through the Secretary of Labour, Robert Reich, is rejecting what he describes as "the diabolical trade-off between good jobs and more jobs", and Singapore, for example, is telling companies in search of low cost labour to call next door to Malaysia or Indonesia.

The White Paper points out that low pay, low skills and low technology are not a sustainable basis for development. Europe, 95 per cent of whose trade is internal, would impoverish itself if it attempted to compete with low costs producers in South East Asia on the basis of wage levels. The challenge for Europe, including Ireland, is to maintain living standards and create more jobs by developing new products, new ideas, new ways of doing things and to compete on the basis of quality, customer orientation and skills.

LESSONS FOR IRELAND

There are three key lessons Ireland can learn from the current debate on Competitiveness and Employment in Europe.

First, we are witnessing the creation of a new economic system with implications for work and life which are just as far reaching as the changes heralded by the industrial revolution. What the steam engine did for physical labour, computers, microelectronics and biotechnology are doing for mental labour today. Today's technological revolution is producing a global society organised around information, knowledge, learning and communications. Irish companies must learn that the knowledge content of a product is the valuable part.

Second, to stay up there with our partners in Europe, we must unleash an innovative process in our culture at every level. To innovate effectively whether it be with products or services or new forms of work based on world class manufacturing requires a high trust environment with workers and their unions accepted by companies as partners in their enterprises. For many Irish companies this in itself may be the biggest and most important innovation they will have to make.

Third, a key feature in the competitive success of German and Japanese companies is the adaptability and flexibility of their management and workers. Adaptability requires security and commitment. This is achieved by workers having a stake in the enterprise and firms taking a longer term view of their investment in the workforce. The belief that flexibility requires insecurity needs to be replaced with the belief that security is essential to flexibility.

ISSUES TO BE ADDRESSED

The European Union, including Ireland, must commit itself firmly to and set its sights on achieving a high wage economy with proper social protection where our competitive advantage is based primarily on the quality and skills of our workforce.

The challenge for Ireland, our trade unions and employers is to develop a vision of ourselves as a high-wage, highly innovative, high-quality, high-skilled society.

Ireland should not seek to compete by reducing social protection and should not follow Britain down that road. Early decisions should be taken on key outstanding proposals under the Social Action Programme in relation to European Workers Council, Atypical Workers, Parental Leave, Protection of Young Workers, Cross-Border Sub-Contracting and Reversal of the Burden of Proof.

The social partners have a key role to play in adapting the European model to the challenges it now faces. Structures, mechanisms and resources must be in place to enable the social partners to effectively contribute to the development and future direction of European economic, social and industrial relations policies. This should be underpinned by the development of social partnership at national level and social partnership at company level.

The need to speed up the pace of adaptation to change, innovation and high technology, requires the development of a high trust environment at company level, with workers and their unions being accepted as partners in the enterprise. While social partnership characterises the relationships between employers and unions at national level, workplace industrial relations are still firmly rooted in the adversarial model. Work is still organised either along Taylorist lines or in line with principles of "hard" HRM as opposed to "soft" HRM.

To remain competitive, companies will have to invest much more on an on-going basis in high-skill training, retraining and technological literacy for all their workers. The industrial relations agenda should be broadened to provide for agreements between unions and employers on these issues at company level.

Our industrial relations procedures need to be continuously updated to ensure that they facilitate adaptation, by workers and management to change, innovation and new technology. The great majority of days lost due to strikes in the past three years arose from disputes involving reorganisation and rationalisation. In most cases, workers were excluded from the decision-making process leading to major change involving redundancy, loss of earnings and the downgrading of permanent full-time employment to part-time and casual working.

References

Ackroyd, S., Burrell, C., Hughes, M. and Whitaker, A. (1988) "The Japanisation of British Industry?", *Industrial Relations Journal*, 19, 1: 11-23.

Ahlstrand, B. W. (1990) *The Quest for Productivity: A Case Study of Fawley after Flanders*, Cambridge: Cambridge University Press.

Ansoff, H. I. (1987) "The emerging paradigm of strategic behaviour", *Strategic Management Journal*, 18, 6: 501-515.

Atkinson, A. J. (1984) *Flexible Manning: The Way Ahead*, London: Institute of Manpower Studies.

Atkinson, J. (1984) "Manpower Strategies for Flexible Organisations", *Personnel Management*, August, 28-31.

Beer, M., Spector, B., Lawrence, P. R., Quinn-Mills, D. and Walton, R. E. (1984) *Managing Human Assets*, New York: The Free Press.

Block, P. (1992) *The Empowered Manager — Positive Political Skills at Work*, San Francisco: Jossey Bass.

Blyton, P. and Turnbull, P. (1992) *Reassessing Human Resource Management*, London: Sage.

Bradley, K. and Hill, S. (1983). "After Japan: The Quality Circle Transplant and Productive Efficiency", *British Journal of Industrial Relations*, 21: 291-311.

Bradley, K. and Hill, S. (1987) "Quality Circles and Managerial Interests", *Industrial Relations*, 26: 68-82.

Brannick, T. and Doyle, L. (1994) "Industrial Conflict" in Murphy, T. and Roche, W. K. (eds.) q.v.

Brewster, C. (1992) "Managing Industrial Relations", in Towers, B (ed.), *A Handbook of Industrial Relations Practice*, London: Kogan Page.

Brewster, C. and Hegewich, A. (1994) *Policy and Practice in European Human Resource Management: The Price Waterhouse Cranfield Survey*, London: Routledge.

Brewster, C., Hegewisch, A., Lockhart, T., and Mayne, L. (1993), *Flexible Working Patterns in Europe*, London: Institute of Personnel Management.

Briggs, P. (1991) "Organisational Commitment — The Key to Japanese Success?", in Brewster, C. and Tyson, S. (eds.) *International Comparisons on Human Resource Management,* London: Pitman.

Buchanan, D. and McCalman, J. (1989*) High Performance Work Systems: The Digital Experience*, London: Routledge.

Clutterbuck, D. (1985) *New Patterns of Work*, London: Pitman.

Collard, R. (1989) *Total Quality: Success Through People*, London: Institute of Personnel Management.

Collard, R. and Dale, B. (1989) "Quality Circles" in K. Sisson (ed.) *Personnel Management in Britain*, Oxford: Blackwell.

Communications Workers' Union (1994) *The Future of the Telecommunications Industry in Ireland*, Dublin: CWU.

Cooper, R. (1977) *Job Motivation and Job Design*, London: Institute of Personnel Management.

Curson, C. (1986) *Flexible Patterns of Work*, London: Institute of Personnel Management.

Daft, R. L. and Buenger, V. (1990) "Hitching a ride on a fast train to nowhere", in Frederickson, J. W. *Perspectives on Strategic Management*, New York: Harper and Row.

Daniel, W. W. (1987) *Workplace Industrial Relations and Technical Change*, London: Pinter.

Dastmalachian, A., Blyton, P. and Adamson, R. (1991) *The Climate of Workplace Relations* London: Routledge.

Department of Labour (1980) *Worker Participation: A Discussion Document*, Dublin: Stationery Office.

Department of Labour (1986) *Advisory Committee on Worker Participation: Report to the Minister of Labour*, Dublin: Stationery Office.

Develin, R. (1989) *The Effectiveness of Quality Improvement Programmes in British Business*, London: Develin and Associates.

Dobbs, J. (1993) "The Empowerment Environment", *Training and Development*, February, 55-57.

Edwards, P. K. and Whitston, C. (1989) "Industrial Discipline, the Control of Attendance, and the Subordination of Labour: Towards an Integrated Analysis", *Work, Employment and Society*, 3: 1-28.

Edwards, P. K. and Whitston, C. (1993) *Attending to Work: The Management of Attendance and Shopfloor Order*, Oxford: Blackwell.

Elger, T. (1990) "Technical Innovation and Work Reorganisation in British Manufacturing in the 1980s: Continuity, Intensification or Transformation?", *Work, Employment and Society*, Special Issue, May: 67-101.

Elger, T. and Fairbrother, P. (1992) "Inflexible Flexibility: A Case Study of Modularization" in *Fordism and Flexibility: Divisions and Change*, N. Gilbert, R. Burrows and A. Pollert (eds.), London: MacMillan.

EOLAS, (1993) *Concluding Statement of the Board*, Dublin: EOLAS, The Irish Science and Technology Agency.

European Foundation for the Improvement of Living and Working Conditions (1993) *Workplace Involvement in Technological Innovation in the European Community*, Dublin: EFILWC.

Feigenbaum, A. (1983) *Total Quality Control*, New York: McGraw-Hill.

Ferner, A. and Hyman, R. (1992) *Industrial Relations in the New Europe*, Oxford: Blackwell.

Fitzgerald, G. (1995) "The European Union and Developments in Industrial Relations", in Gunnigle, P., McMahon, G. V. and Fitzgerald, G., q.v.

Flood, P. (1989) "Human Resource Management: Promise, Possibility and Limitations" unpublished research paper, University of Limerick.

Flood, P. (1990) "Atypical Employment: Core-Periphery Manpower Strategies — the Implications for Corporate Culture" *Industrial Relations News Report*, 9: 16-18; 10: 17-20.

Fombrun, C. (1986) "Environmental trends create new pressures on human resources" in Rynes, S. L. and Milkovich, G. T. *Current Issues in Human Resource Management*, Plano, Texas: Business Publications Inc.

Fox, A. (1974) *Man Mismanagement*, London: Hutchinson.

Garavan, T. and Morley, M. (1992) "Organisational Change and Development" in *Case Studies in HRM*, London: Institute of Personnel Management.

Geary, J. F. (1993) "New Forms of Work Organization: The Case of Two American Electronics Plants: Plural, Mixed and Protean", *Economic and Industrial Democracy*, 14, 4: 511-534.

Geary, J. F. (1994) "New Forms of Work Organisation: Implications for Employers, Trade Unions and Employees", Working Paper No. 9, Graduate School of Business, University College Dublin.

Geary, J. F. (1994) "Task Participation: Employees' Participation Enabled or Constrained?" in *Personnel Management: A Comprehensive Guide to Theory and Practice in Britain*, K. Sisson (ed.). Oxford: Basil Blackwell.

Gribbin, R. (1992) "Rover Men Agree to 'Japanese' Work Deal", *Daily Telegraph*, 14 April, 9.

Gunnigle, P. (1994) "Collectivism and the Management of Industrial Relations in Greenfield Sites", paper presented to the International Industrial Relations Association European Congress, Helsinki, August.

Gunnigle, P. and Daly, A. (1992) "Craft Integration and Flexible Work Practices", *Journal of Industrial and Commercial Training*, 24: 10-17.

Gunnigle, P., Flood, P., Morley, M. and Turner, T. (1994) *Continuity and Change in Irish Employee Relations,* Dublin: Oak Tree Press.

Gunnigle, P., McMahon, G. V. and Fitzgerald, G. (1995) *Industrial Relations in Ireland: Theory and Practice,* Dublin: Gill and Macmillan (forthcoming).

Gunnigle, P., and Morley, M. (1993) "Something Old — Something New: A Perspective on Industrial Relations in the Republic of Ireland", *Review of Employment Topics*, 1, 1: 114-142.

Guth, W. D. and MacMillan, I. C. (1989) "Strategy implementation versus middle management self-interest" in *Readings in Strategic Management*, Asch, D. (ed.) London: MacMillan.

Hackman, J.R. and Oldham, G.R. (1980) *Work Redesign*, New York: Addison-Wesley.

Handy, C. (1990) *The Age of Unreason,* London: Century Hutchinson.

Hannaway, C. (1987) "New Style Collective Agreements: An Irish Approach", *Industrial Relations News Report*, 13, 16-22.

Hannaway, C. (1992) "Why Irish Eyes are Smiling", *Personnel Management*, 38-41.

Hardiman, N. (1988) *Pay, Politics and Economic Performance in Ireland, 1970-1987*, Oxford: Clarendon Press.

Hardscombe, R. S. and Norman, P. A. (1989) *Strategic Leadership: The Missing Link*, London: McGraw-Hill.

Harrison, H. (1992) *Developing Human Resources for Productivity*, Geneva: International Labour Organisation.

Harrison, R. (1992) *Employee Development,* London: Institute of Personnel Management.

Hastings, T. (1994) *Semi-States in Crisis: The Challenge for Industrial Relations in the ESB and Other Major Semi-State Companies*, Dublin: Oak Tree Press.

Hill, S. (1991) "Why Quality Circles Failed but Total Quality Management Might Succeed", *British Journal of Industrial Relations*, 29: 541-568.

Hoerr, J. Pollock, M., and Whiteside, D. (1986) "Management Discovers the Human Side of Automation", *Business Week*, September, 60-65.

Hogg, C. (1990) *Total Quality*, London: Institute of Personnel Management, Factsheet No. 29.

Hourihan, F. (1994) "The European Union and Industrial Relations," in Murphy, T. and Roche, W. K. (eds.) q.v.

Hyman, R. (1994) "Industrial Relations in Western Europe: An Era of Ambiguity?", *Industrial Relations*, 33, 1: 1-24.

Income Data Services (1988) *Teamworking*, IDS Study 419, London: IDS.

Industrial Policy Review Group (J. Culliton, chair) (1992) *A Time for Change: Industrial Policy for the 1990s*, Dublin:The Stationery Office.

Industrial Relations News (1993) "Restructuring and Culture Change to Meet Today's Realtiy: Industrial Relations Conference Report", Dublin: IRN.

Industrial Relations News Report (1994), 48; (1995), 2;4.

Irish Congress of Trade Unions (1993) *New Forms of Work Organisation: Options for Unions*, Dublin: ICTU.

Johnson, G. and Scholes, K. (1993) *Exploring Corporate Strategy*, London: Prentice-Hall.

Jones, B. (1988) "Work and Flexible Automation in Britain: A Review of Developments and Possibilities", *Work, Employment and Society*, 2, 4: 451-86.

Katzenbach, J. and Smith, D. (1992) *The Wisdom of Teams: Creating the High Performance Organization*, Boston: Harvard Business School Press.

Keenan, J. and Thom, A. (1988) "The Future Through the Keyhole: Some Thoughts on Employment Patterns", *Personnel Review*, 17: 20-24.

Kelly, A. and Brannick, T. (1988) "The Management of Human Resources: New Trends and the Challenge to Trade Unions", *Arena*, August, pp. 11-25.

Kelly, J. and Kelly, C. (1991) "'Them and Us': Social Psychology and 'The New Industrial Relations'", *British Journal of Industrial Relations*, 29: 25-48.

Kennedy, K. A., Giblin, T. and McHugh, D. (1988) *The Economic Development of Ireland in the Twentieth Century,* London: Routledge.

Klein, J., (1989) "The Human Cost of Manufacturing Reform", *Harvard Business Review*, Mar/Apr, pp. 60-66.

Klein, J. A. (1991) "A Reexamination of Autonomy in Light of New Manufacturing Practices", *Human Relations*, 44, 1: 21-38.

Kochan T. and Dyer, L. (1993) "Managing Transformational Change: The Role of Human Resource Professionals", *International Journal of Human Resource Management*, 3: 569-90.

Lawler, E. (1986) *High Involvement Management: Participative Strategies for Organizational Performance*, San Francisco: Jossey Bass.

Marchington, M. (1982) *Managing Industrial Relations*, London: McGraw-Hill.

Marchington, M. and Parker, P. (1990) *Changing Patterns of Employee Relations*, Hemel Hempstead: Harvester Wheatsheaf.

Marginson, P. (1992) "European Integration and Transnational Management-Union Relations in the Enterprise", *British Journal of Industrial Relations,* 30, 4: 529-545.

Marsden, D. and Thompson, M. (1990) "Flexibility Agreements and Their Significance in the Increases in Productivity in British Manufacturing since 1980" in *Work, Employment and Society*, 4: 83-104.

McAleese, D. and Gallagher, M. (1994) "Developments in Irish Trade During the 1980s", in M. Lambkin and T. Meenaghan, (eds.), *Perspectives on Marketing Management in Ireland*, Dublin: Oak Tree Press.

McLoughlin, I. (1990) "Management, Work Organization and CAD — Towards Flexible Automation?", *Work, Employment and Society*, 4, 2: 217-237.

McLoughlin, I. and Clark, J. (1988) *Technological Change at Work*, Milton Keynes: Open University Press.

McMahon, G. V. (1995) "New Work Organisation and Quality Initiatives", in Gunnigle, P., McMahon, G. V. and Fitzgerald, G., q. v.

Mooney, P. (1989) *The Growth of the Non-Union Sector and Union Counter Strategies,* unpublished PhD, Trinity College, Dublin.

Morley, M. and Garavan, T. (1993) "The New Organisation — It's Implications for Training and Development", paper read to the 24th National Conference of the Irish Institute of Training and Development, Galway, April.

Morrissey, T.J. (1989) "Employee Participation at Sub-Board Level", in *Industrial Relations in Ireland: Contemporary Issues and Developments*, Dublin: Department of Industrial Relations,University College Dublin.

Moss Kanter, R. (1983) *The Change Masters: Corporate Entrepreneurs at Work*, London and Boston: Unwin.

Murphy, T. and Roche, W. K. (eds.) (1994) *Irish Industrial Relations in Practice*, Dublin: Oak Tree Press.

Murray, S. (1984) *Industrial Relations in Irish Private Sector Manufacturing Industry,* Dublin: Industrial Development Authority.

National Economic and Social Council (1993) *A Strategy for Competitiveness, Growth and Employment*, Dublin: NESC, Paper No. 96.

Pendleton, A. (1991) "The Barriers to Flexibility: Flexible Rostering on the Railways", *Work, Employment and Society*, 5, 2: 241-257.

Perry, B. (1984) *Einfield: A High Performance System*, Bedford, MA: Digital Equipment Corporation Educational Services Development and Publishing.

Piore, M. and Sabel, C. (1984) *The Second Industrial Divide: Possibilities for Prosperity*, New York: Basic Books.

Proctor, S. J., Rowlinson, M., McArdle, L., Hassard, J. and Forrester, P. (1994) "Flexibility, Politics and Strategy: In Defence of the Model of the Flexible Firm", *Work, Employment and Society*, 8: 221-42.

Purcell, J. (1991) "The Impact of Corporate Strategy on Human Resource Management", in Storey, J. (ed), *New Perspectives on Human Resource Management*, London: Routledge.

Quinn-Mills, D. (1991) *The Rebirth of the Corporation*, New York: Wiley.

Regalia. E. (1994) *The Positions of the Social Partners on Direct Participation in Europe*, Milano: IRES Lombardia, Employee Direct Participation in Organisational Change — The EPOC Project.

Rhodes, M. (1992) "The Future of the Social Dimension: Labour Market Regulation in Post 1992 Europe", *Journal of Common Market Studies,* 30, 1: 23-51.

Roche, W. K. (1994a) "Pay Determination, The State and the Politics of Industrial Relations" in Murphy T. and Roche, W. K. (eds.), q.v.

Roche, W. K. (1994b) "The Trend of Unionisation" in Murphy, T. and Roche, W. K. (eds.), q.v.

Roche, W. K. and Geary, J. (1994) "The Attenuation of Host-Country Effects? Multinationals, Industrial Relations and Collective Bargaining in Ireland", working paper, Business Research Programme, Graduate School of Business, University College Dublin.

Roche, W. K. and Turner, T. (1994) "Testing Alternative Models of Human Resource Policy Effects on Trade Union Recognition in the Republic of Ireland", *International Journal of Human Resource Management*, 5: 721-53.

Rose, M. (1975) *Industrial Behaviour — Theoretical Developments since Taylor*, London: Pelican Books.

Rubery, J. (1992) "Pay, Gender and the Social Dimension to Europe", *British Journal of Industrial Relations,* 30, 4: 605-621

Salamon, M. (1992) *Industrial Relations: Theory and Practice*, London: Prentice-Hall..

Schuler, R. and Jackson, S. (1987) "Organisational strategy and organisational level as determinants of HRM practices", *Human Resource Planning*, 10, 3: 125-141.

Services, Industrial and Professional Trade Union (1993) "Discussion Paper Series C", unpublished, Dublin: SIPTU Research Department.

Sewell, G. and Wilkinson, B. (1992) "Employment or Emasculation? Shopfloor Surveillance in a Total Quality Organisation" in Blyton, P. and Turnbull, P. (eds.), *Reassessing Human Resource Management*, London: Sage.

Shepard, H.A. (1967) "Innovation Resisting and Innovation Producing Organisation", *Journal of Business*, 40: 470-477.

Smith, C., Child, J. and Rowlinson, M. (1990) *Reshaping Work: The Cadbury Experience*, Cambridge: Cambridge University Press.

Storey, J. (1992) *Developments in the Management of Human Resources*, Oxford: Blackwell.

Streeck, W. (1985) *Industrial Relations and Industrial Adjustment in the Motor Industry*, public lecture, Industrial Relations Research Unit, University of Warwick.

Streeck, W. (1992) "Productive Constraints: On the Institutional Conditions of Diversified Quality Production", in *Social Institutions and Economic Performance*, London: Sage.

Suttle, S. (1988) "Labour Market Flexibility", *Industrial Relations News Report*, 38: 13-16.

Tailby, S. and Whitston, C. (1989) "Industrial Relations and Restructuring", in *Manufacturing Change: Industrial Relations and Restructuring*, S. Tailby and C. Whitston (eds.), Oxford: Basil Blackwell.

Thompson, R.T. (1991) "The Changing Character of Employee Relations", *Journal of Labour Research*, 12, 4: 240-262.

Tiernan, S. (1993) "Organisational Transformation: The Case of Team Aer Lingus", mimeo, Department of Management, University of Limerick.

Toffler, A. (1971) *Future Shock*, New York: Penguin.

Toffler, A. (1980) *The Third Wave*, New York: Penguin.

Turnbull, P. (1988) "The Limits To 'Japanisation' — Just-In-Time, Labour Relations and the U.K. Automotive Industry", *New Technology, Work and Employment*, 3: 7-20.

Turnbull, P. J. (1989) "Industrial Restructuring and Labour Relations in the Automotive Components Industry: 'Just-in-Time' or 'Just-too-Late'?" in *Manufacturing Change: Industrial Relations and Restructuring*, S. Tailby and C. Whitston (eds.), Oxford: Basil Blackwell.

Turner, L. (1991) *Democracy at Work: Changing World Markets and the Future of Labour Unions*, Ithaca, NY: Cornell University Press.

Vaill, P. (1992) "The Purposing of High Performance Systems", *Organisational Dynamics*, Autumn, 23-29.

Wall, et al. (1986) "Outcomes of Autonomous Work Groups: A Long-Term Field Experiment", *Academy of Management Journal*, 29, 2: 280-304.

Whelan, C. (1982) *Worker Priorities, Trust in Management and Prospects for Worker Participation*, Dublin: Economic and Social Research Institute, Paper No. 111.

Wickens, P. (1987) *The Road to Nissan: Flexibility, Quality and Teamwork*, London: Macmillan.

Wickham, J. (1993) *New Forms of Work in Ireland: An Analysis of the "New Forms of Work and Activity" Data Set*, Dublin: European Foundation for the Improvement of Living and Working Conditions, Working Paper No. WP/93/31/EN.

Wilkinson, A. (1992) "Fitness for Use? Barriers to Full TQM in the U.K.", *Management Decision* 29.

Wilkinson, A., Redman, T. and Snape, E. (1993) *Quality and the Manager*, London: Institute of Management.

Wilkinson, B. and Oliver, N. (1990) "Obstacles to Japanization: The Case of Ford UK", *Employee Relations*, 12 (1): 17-21.

Willener, A. (1970) *The Action Image of Society*, London: Tavistock Institute of Human Relations.

Williams, A., Dobson, P. and Walters, M. (1989) *Changing Cultures: New Organisational Approaches*, London: Institute of Personnel Management.

Woolridge, B. and Floyd, S. W. (1990) "The Strategy Process: Middle management involvement and organisational performance", *Strategic Management Journal*, 11: 231-241.